*It's Your Life...Live IT!* perfectly captures the evolution of Gutsy Women and our mission to start a company that catered to women who were underserved in the travel market. Through the stories portrayed of women sharing how their trips have been life-changing, April's book provides inspiration to women everywhere to be resilient, to never give up, and to take time for self-care and renewal.

~ Gail Golden-Icahn, cofounder Gutsy Women Travel

I had the great pleasure and adventure of being on one of April's trips—this one, to Costa Rica. This gutsy entrepreneur has much to share, not only about the exhilaration of travel, but on jetting out of our comfort zones and into new friendships and enhanced self-discovery.

~ Iris Krasnow, *New York Times* best-selling author of *Secret Lives of Wives.*

*It's Your Life...Live IT!* is a captivating and eloquent memoir that provides insight into the author's vision, aspirations, struggles, and victories both in the business world and in academia.

~Reverend Father Kyrian C. Echekwu, PhD

*It's Your Life...Live IT!* takes you on April Merenda's many leaps of faith throughout her career and believing in herself. It's no surprise that Gutsy Women Travel is a success...a success because she hung on when others let go! April teaches her hospitality students with the same drive and motivation. She has inspired me to work hard and dream big and most important to believe in myself.

~Kate Smith, Manager of Faculty Support, St. John's University School of Law, CCPS '21, MSIHM '22

April's story is inspiring and courageous. She is the personification of what a "gutsy woman" is. I'm delighted to have traveled on eighteen Gutsy Women tours and every one of them has enriched my life while enabling me to meet incredible people along the way.

~ Montez Long, aka Monty Gutsy Woman of the Year 2017

# It's Your Life...
# Live IT!

THE STORY OF BUILDING A TRAVEL BUSINESS AFTER
9/11 AND HOW IT SURVIVED A GLOBAL PANDEMIC
WITH LESSONS LEARNED ALONG THE WAY.

### April M. Merenda

the three
tomatoes
The Three Tomatoes Book Publishing

Published November 2021

ISBN: 978-1-7376177-3-0

Library of Congress Control Number: 2021921154

For information address:
The Three Tomatoes Book Publishing
6 Soundview Rd.
Glen Cove, NY 11542


Cover design: Susan Herbst and Dick Basmagy
Interior design: Susan Herbst

## *Dedication*

In memory of Gilda Merenda, my beautiful mother who taught me
many lessons, the most important of which are
to be kind, empathetic, and gutsy.

A portion of the proceeds from the book will be donated to
the MJHS Hospice Foundation.

# Table of Contents

# *Foreword*

After spending decades in the travel industry traversing the globe more times than I could count, I felt great joy and much anticipation to help launch the brand Gutsy Women Travel in the fall of 2001, two months after the senseless attacks on September 11, 2001.

The idea of a travel company dedicated to marketing to women travelers was certainly innovative at the time, but the concept seemed natural to me after having been raised by an amazing mother who immigrated to America from Italy in 1937 to pursue a better life. What's more, throughout my teenage and adult years, I was surrounded by powerful women—sisters, cousins, amazing college friends, and co-workers—who came to my aid when life threw curveballs my way. To this day, I continue to have incredible female friends and family members who are always there when I need them.

Looking back over my many trips and recalling events that affected those trips, certainly the horrendous attacks on 9/11 stand out, and stranded many of us in worldwide places for days and weeks. Personally, I've lived through some unusual experiences and witnessed firsthand historical events.

For instance, fast-forward a decade after 9/11 to January 2011, my Gutsy Women group and I were part of the largest evacuation of U.S. citizens at that time over a forty-eight-hour period from Cairo, Egypt after being caught up in the middle of the Arab Spring revolution that eventually overthrew the regime of President Mubarak.

To a lesser extent, I've been stuck in the Dakotas for days due to very poor weather conditions. Further back in time when I lived in Hawaii in 1979, I couldn't get back to the mainland because all DC-10 aircraft were grounded due to concerns about the aircraft's serious equipment flaws!

But never could I, or anyone else, have imagined that a virus, COVID-19, would kill over four and a half million people globally and literally shut down the world. In all my years in the travel business would I have imagined a scenario that would shut down worldwide leisure travel. No planes. No trains. No ships.

I live in the suburbs of New York City and watched in horror as the city became the epicenter for the virus. In the first three months of the pandemic in 2020, more than 203,000 people had tested positive. Our hospitals were overloaded with COVID patients, and our health care workers were extended to the limits. Thousands of New Yorkers died during that period alone.

There was limited subway and bus service. I saw colleagues who worked in the travel business lose their jobs and witnessed businesses, such as the iconic Roosevelt Hotel and Hilton Times Square in New York City shut their doors forever.

I am also an assistant professor/industry professional at St. John's University in New York. On March 7, the school closed its doors and went to remote learning. I didn't return to campus until fall 2020.

The year 2020 was the year the Earth stood still for everyone, including me and my Gutsy Women travelers, my family, and my students.

It was a difficult time for everyone, and like many people, I became depressed with the sickness and death all around us and being confined to our homes for months. I was heartbroken that I had to cancel all the trips that Gutsy Women Travel had offered in 2020 through mid-June of 2021, but I hoped and prayed that the invisible monster, COVID-19, would be vanquished. I lamented that my world travels and adventures of experiencing new cultures and tasting different foods was taken from me. The weather in New York didn't help either—a hot summer and a cold, snowy winter. And then in November of 2020, my ninety-nine-year-old heroine mother who was in hospice care in her home passed away. What more heartache could 2020 bring? I thought.

But spring 2021 brought a spring to my step too. I had survived the pandemic and am now among the legions of vaccinated people. Many destinations are slowly opening their doors. One sage wrote that planning a trip elevates a woman's soul and can be the best antidote to the depression that all of us experienced during the pandemic. I tested this theory and flew to Florida in April 2021 after fifteen months of not traveling. What a feeling of freedom to be on a plane, walk through an airport, and feel the warmth of the Florida sun. I felt renewed.

I continued my journey of renewal by leading a group of women on the Gutsy Women Iceland Explorer trip in June 2021, our first trip since the onset of the pandemic in March 2020. It was a wonderful experience for all as we shed the mental and physical remnants of COVID-19, soaking and relaxing in the thermal waters at Retreat Spa Blue Lagoon, wondering at the cascading waters of the stunning Skógafoss waterfalls and sailing among the jagged icebergs in the Jökulsárlón Glacier Lagoon.

It was in this beautiful, serene, and healing environment, surrounded by gutsy women who were so joyful to be traveling again, that it suddenly hit me like a thunderbolt: my twenty-year-old company, Gutsy Women Travel, had survived the pandemic, and we're ready to travel and explore the world again.

It's been an incredible journey and I've learned a lot along the way, both business and life lessons. This is my story.

*April M. Merenda*

# 1

## *You're Not in Brooklyn Anymore*

I've always believed in signs from the universe, and it was a phone call out of the blue in May 1999 that was about to change my life. But before we get to that turning point, let me back up a bit.

I'm a first-generation Italian American girl from Brooklyn, whose family emigrated to the U.S. from Salerno, Italy hoping for a better life like so many before them. I inherited many good traits from my parents, including a strong work ethic, loyalty, and a love for family and friends. But my gutsy DNA comes from my mother, Gilda, who was feisty and gutsy right up until her passing on November 29, 2020, just shy of her one hundredth birthday that was to be celebrated on February 21, 2021.

Brooklyn is a great place, but I also knew the world was a much bigger place than Brooklyn, and I wanted to see it all. When I was four, my family moved to Long Island. I worked hard at Maria Regina High School in Uniondale, and then was awarded a full four-year scholarship in public speaking and debate to St. John's University in Queens, New York. I earned a bachelor of science degree in criminal justice in 1975, and then took the law boards with the intention of going to law school. My parents were thrilled. My uncle, Judge Nicholas Silletti went to St. John's University School of Law and he was the classmate and debate partner of Governor Mario Cuomo.

St. John's did not offer degrees in hospitality until twenty-four years later, so the field never occurred to me, and internships in any field were uncommon. So, like many other students, I waitressed during my college years, and planned to do so the summer I graduated while I waited to get into law school.

And then fate stepped in. Or as the lyric from John Lennon's "Beautiful Boy," says, "Life is what happens to you while you're busy making other plans."

The owner of the Ole London Fishery, a restaurant I had worked in near St. John's, offered me the chance to be the manager of his new restaurant, Uncle Fish, in Cedarhurst, Long Island. One night a man came in who was a pilot for the charter division of TWA Airlines. He became a regular and we often chatted. Toward the end of the summer, he mentioned they were working with leading tour operators to take groups to Las Vegas. I was intrigued. He told me who to contact, and after interviewing, I was offered a job selling show tickets and tours right on the plane. The great part was that I could stay in Vegas for a couple of days each trip and take in various shows and sights. That personal experience helped me improve my sales pitch. This was my first job in the travel business, and it was a great opportunity. I became the company's highest ticket seller. It was fun and exciting.

On one of the flights, I met a colleague of Jilly Rizzo, a colorful restaurateur and best buddy to Frank Sinatra. We chatted and before we landed, he wrote on a cocktail napkin, admit two to Frank Sinatra's show at Caesars Palace, and told me to see his colleague at the hotel's VIP desk. Taking a leap of faith, I alerted my girlfriend who lived in Vegas and that night we exchanged the cocktail napkin for two VIP seats to see Sinatra. That was my start in the hospitality business, and I never looked back.

That job led to my next one working as a tour manager with other charter groups that were organized through Classic Tours and Travel. They specialized in twelve-night vacation packages to San Francisco, Hawaii, and Las Vegas. I traveled with the tour to each of those places for the duration of the trip. After a few months, management decided it would be more cost-effective and less wear and tear on me, to base me in Hawaii. They would use local tour managers to oversee the tours in San Francisco and Las Vegas.

They provided me with housing at the Holiday Inn Waikiki where the tour groups stayed. I had a beautiful one-bedroom suite with a living room overlooking the ocean. It was a wonderful experience. I got to see amazing entertainment like Elvis Presley, Don Ho, and the Kodak Hula Show. I visited Pearl Harbor and the many glorious beaches in Honolulu. I got to visit all the other islands on the optional tours we offered. It was a dream job, but I soon learned it wasn't all fun and glamour.

Part of my job was to meet the charter groups in the hotel lobby of the Holiday Inn Waikiki. Upon their arrival, I would tell them about the day-to-day itinerary and optional tours, and let them know they were free until their Hawaiian luau welcome dinner. About two hours after one group's arrival, I received a phone call from the front desk. One of my clients had a heart attack on the beach directly across from our hotel and passed away. His wife fainted at the scene and paramedics were taking her to the hospital. The hotel needed to reach someone in their family and needed my help.

Fortunately, when I chatted with the couple at the arrival briefing, they told me they were there to celebrate their twenty-fifth wedding anniversary, and I remembered them mentioning seeing their son who was in the military and was based at Schofield Barracks in O'ahu. Thank goodness the hotel was able to reach him. This was the first time I realized you had to be resilient and resourceful in this business.

I lived in Hawaii for almost a year, and then group travel was affected with the DC-10 groundings. By then island fever had set in, and I wanted to get back to the mainland. Just prior to the holiday season in 1979, I returned to New York. Thanks to my dear friend Susan Wilson, who I met at St. John's University, I was able to rent a one-bedroom apartment on Riverside Drive and Seventy-Ninth Street. As we entered 1980, the U.S. economy had its challenges and they adversely affected the travel industry.

As I contemplated my next career move, I remembered the words of one of my wise professors at St. John's University. He stressed that when the economy is bad in one part of the world, it often benefits another part of the world. While the low dollar exchange rate and high gas prices led to fewer Americans traveling, the European travel market to the U.S. was flourishing. That's when I knew the direction I should pursue.

I saw many advertisements by tour operators handling European tourists to New York City. I reached out to one of them, Soljet Tours, which at that time was located at 1500 Broadway. I was immediately hired as operations manager. Attending law school was now a distant memory.

All of their employees had international backgrounds. As the only native New Yorker, my job was to assist with organizing tours and transportation for visiting groups to New York City, and to make sure everything went off without a hitch. I loved the job and also meeting the visiting tourists who came mainly from Germany, the Netherlands, and Spain.

In the summer of that year, I was assigned a huge project to organize tours for a very large group traveling from Germany to New York via a chartered Russian ship, the *Maksim Gorkiy*, set to arrive in September. The group was organized by Neckermann Reizen in Germany. Their clients expressed interest in walking tours through Central Park, seeing a show at Radio City and off Broadway, going to Harlem to experience a singing gospel mass, seeing traditional sites like the Empire State Building, and one-day flights to see Niagara Falls. I was more than up to the task with my tourism industry experience and with my New York roots, I rose to the challenge. But then I was thrown an obstacle that tested my resiliency at the ripe age of twenty-six years young!

The *Maksim Gorkiy* ship had her share of politics that September 1980. She was denied permission to enter the port of New York City as a reaction of the U.S. to the Russian invasion of Afghanistan that same year. She had to anchor off Staten Island and her hundreds of passengers were ferried ashore to New York City. The front page of every New York newspaper pictured the ship, anchored at sea with its hammer and sickle country logo made from tons of iron, boldly displayed. Union ship members and other patriots were pictured pouring Russian vodka into the Hudson River.

It was a riveting time, especially for me, as I was responsible for organizing the bus transportation to and from the many optional tours we had painstakingly confirmed for the hundreds of German passengers traveling on that ship. We had to now allow lead in travel time from the launches to arrive on shore and then board them on buses to the various excursions. This was not a simple task.

I pulled it off and learned a lot about myself and a lot about the German people. Some of them were elderly, but they never complained. They were strong-willed, and I marveled at their agility and stamina. I loved hearing their stories and at the same time showing them the wonders of New York City. Just a year prior, the "I♥NY" campaign was released and despite how the ship was forced to dock outside our New York City port, every tourist left that trip loving New York.

One thing that the women cruise passengers marveled about was my clothing style, which developed over that time thanks to my mother, Gilda, who was a seamstress by trade.

Gilda was excited that I had my first job in the Big Apple but knew that after paying rent for a one-bedroom apartment, there wasn't much left from my paycheck each month. When I would visit my parents on weekends at their Long Island home, my mother would always surprise me with an outfit she made from material remnants she bought on sale. At the time, I was five feet two and a half inches (I always have to get that half in there). I wore a kitten heel with most of my outfits, which complemented the designs she made for me. Today I'm five feet one inch. Yes, I've shrunk.

The cruise passengers also commented on my scent, which was Chanel No. 5. I was introduced to that scent by my brother Eddie who brought me a bottle from one of his trips abroad when he was in the air force. It's still my signature scent to this day.

When I would show up to dispatch the tours for the passengers on the *Maksim Gorkiy*, the women would touch my lace shirts or corduroy jumper or belted velour T-shirt dress and ask where they could buy them in Manhattan. They were in awe when I told them they were handmade by mother who hailed from Salerno, Italy. Maybe it was the fact that they also loved my Italian roots that I became a welcome and comforting sight during their New York stay. When I joined them on the ship to Bermuda, a surprise bonus, it was like I was part of the family!

My boss, Rolf Van Deurzen, who hailed from Holland, was one of the angels in my life. He entrusted me with this project along with his talented team, and I did not disappoint them. On the day the ship was leaving New York to head to Bermuda, he met me with a wonderful surprise. As a bonus for all my arduous efforts, he had arranged for me to sail to Bermuda with the group and had made reservations for me in Hamilton for the weekend at a lovely bed-and-breakfast. He also handed me a cash bonus for travel expenses and a return airline ticket to JFK.

What a job and life I was living...all to prepare me for my move in

1982 to California for the Dutch company Martinair Holland, a charter and cargo airline operating flights to Amsterdam. I was relocated to Los Angeles to open up their Western Regional office. Soon afterward in 1985, I was hired by the number one German tour operator DER (Deutsches Reisebüro) Tours as its Western Regional sales director selling charter flights to Germany on Condor Charters as well as their distribution of Eurail Passes. One of my biggest accomplishments was to secure the AAA travel account that facilitated its travel offices to issue European rail passes to their clientele.

I bought my first house in Ventura, California in 1988 and continued to excel in my travel career. In 1996 I was appointed the first female Italian American to be president of one of the oldest Italian travel companies CIT Tours (Compagnia Italiana Turismo). I worked for them for three years and traveled to Italy three to four times a year. In addition to brushing up on my Italian, I really got to know Italy. My father had passed away in 1993, so I would often take my mother with me on my trips to Italy. She got to see her Italian family and I got to see my mother in her element. Life was good.

Then came that fateful day in May 1999. A headhunter called me totally out of the blue and said he had the perfect job for me. A well-known fifty-year-old travel company was looking for someone with my expertise to rejuvenate an older brand and make it relevant to more travelers. I was intrigued. *Where is it?* I inquired.

This dream job was in Lawrence, Kansas. Here I was, a transplanted New Yorker still not totally comfortable in California, but Kansas? The headhunter also shared that someone big, who he couldn't name, was about to buy the company and that would eventually get me back to my beloved family and friends in New York.

I agreed to fly to Kansas where they offered me the job of vice president of sales and marketing for a venerable travel tour company called Maupintour, well-known for its "people to people" program where travelers would meet with locals. Today the concept of the "people to people" program lives on.

I had some trepidations about the move, but I took a leap of faith, listening to my inner self rather than outside commentary, and accepted the job offer.

There were signs that all roads were leading to Kansas. I rented my house in Ventura, California to, believe it or not, a couple from

Kansas. My moving day was scheduled for August 15, 1999, which ironically, was the sixtieth anniversary of when *The Wizard of Oz* premiered in New York City. I clicked my ruby-red shoes, and there I was in Lawrence, Kansas. But not for long.

It turns out Lawrence is a quaint vibrant college town, and I enjoyed many football games at Kansas University. Even though this Brooklyn girl stuck out like a sore thumb, I was appreciated for my contributions to the company.

The big buyer was big indeed. It was Carl Icahn, the billionaire entrepreneur and founder of Icahn Associates, a diversified conglomerate holding company based in New York City, and one of Wall Street's most successful investors. In November 1999, I clicked my ruby-red heels again, and I was back in New York at Icahn Associates' corporate offices as vice president of sales and marketing for his various travel companies, which now included Maupintour. He also owned TWA at that time, which was another one of the many "coincidences" in my life since my travel career had started with TWA Charters.

# 2

## *Gutsy Women Is Born and Almost Dies Before Launch*

I'll never forget my first day at Icahn Associates. It was November 24, 1999, and it was my birthday. I walked into my office overlooking Fifth Avenue and there was a gift from Henri Bendel's on my desk. The card read *Happy Birthday and welcome back to New York*, signed by Gail Golden, vice president of Icahn Associates and chairman of Lowestfare.com. Gail was to be my manager, but little did I know at the time that she would also become one of my angels. I couldn't believe with everything going on that she took notice that it was my birthday. But if you knew Gail, you wouldn't be surprised. She is the quintessential master of gift giving with a heart of gold.

In mid-December, I found out while speaking to Gail from the US-TOA (United States Tour Operators Association) convention I was attending in Maui that she and Carl Icahn were getting married! I had bought her special votive candles for the holidays and asked her to retrieve them from my desk drawer. I was pleased to learn she placed them around their apartment for the intimate ceremony.

On the same call, she asked if I could go on our Maupintour Millennium trip to Egypt and report back on the quality of our tour operation. So I spent the last week of 1999 experiencing one of the most fascinating countries, on a trip of a lifetime, ringing in the new millennium from the Mena House Hotel in the shadow of the pyramids. (This would not be my last encounter with Egypt.) What a year...what a life!

*April M. Merenda*

In addition to being gracious and generous, Gail Golden-Icahn is incredibly smart. I was handling sales and marketing for Maupintour and was working with Gail on the other travel businesses, which included Lowestfare.com, one of the first online airline ticket booking websites.

Icahn Associates launched the Lowestfare.com website in 1996 as a way to sell the deeply discounted TWA tickets he had received as part of his buyout deal with TWA. I will leave it to the business historians to dissect the demise of TWA. However, Carl had always been a visionary and with the creation of Lowestfare.com he was one of the pioneers in online ticket reservations, along with Travelocity and Expedia, which also launched that year. Lowestfare.com became the basis for what is Priceline.com today.

I was excited to help grow this innovative business concept by creating partnerships with travel agents. What was such a novel business idea at the time soon became the norm for how airline tickets are purchased.

But the real excitement for me was when Carl challenged Gail to come up with new ways for people to travel. He felt that after fifty years, Maupintour needed some new ideas. Gail knew that marketing new products was my strong suit, and she asked me to do some research and come up with some thoughts.

I started to look at the types of travelers and market segments tour companies were targeting. There was family travel, adventure travel, solo travel, and the LGBT market. But there was one market that was glaringly ignored, and that was women travelers.

In 1999, our research found that 20 percent of women over the age of forty were single, divorced, or widowed. A survey of married women found that 50 percent took an annual trip without their spouse for a variety of reasons. Some spouses had different vacation schedules or more time off (like teachers), different interests, or the wife just wanted to travel on her own. No one was speaking specifically to this market segment. I knew there could be an opportunity here, and I was proven right. This segment of women travelers has continued to grow. Today over 50 percent of women over the age of forty are single, divorced, or widowed and continue to travel.

As our team was researching this market, a special shout-out goes to David Lovely and Rob Koch. These "gutsy guys" came across an inspiring book written by Marybeth Bond, a consultant to CBS, called *Gutsy Women*. The book is about how she quit her job to travel the globe for two years. She returned to San Francisco feeling exhilarated and eventually married a man she had crossed paths with on her travel journey. Kismet!

Our sales and marketing meeting was coming up soon and would take place at the Stratosphere Hotel in Las Vegas, which at that time was owned by Carl. I contacted Marybeth to be our guest speaker and she accepted. She was excellent.

On the flight back to New York with Gail and Carl on his private plane, we talked about my research on the women's market and Marybeth's presentation. They suggested I reach out to Marybeth about buying the rights to the name "Gutsy Women." When that had been accomplished, Gail asked for my assistance to help create the travel concept for women around the name using the travel destination experience Maupintour brought to the table. And that was the start of Gutsy Women Travel.

Working closely with Maupintour's product team, especially Mary Nichols, we came up with destinations where every trip would have a unique feature that women could not do on their own. We also limited our travel groups to no more than sixteen women. We agreed that everything that should be essential on a trip would be included in the price, so there were no surprises. All that women really needed was extra spending money for incidentals and out-of-pocket expenses.

The first trip we planned was a walking tour through the Cotswolds and Bath, England. It had a literary focus featuring powerful gutsy women like Jane Austen, who lived and wrote in Bath for years. The trip was unique and delivered on our Gutsy Women brand promise: trips for women about women. We hadn't formally launched but several women had already expressed interest.

And then 9/11 happened. Like everyone, that day is forever etched in my memory. Our offices were in the former General Motors building on the corner of Fifty-Ninth Street and Fifth Avenue. We didn't know what was going to happen next, and if our building, which was one of the tallest in midtown Manhattan and hosted several financial services firms, would be under attack. It was a terrifying time.

When we returned to the office a few days later, Carl called a meeting for the travel division. He thought travel would be affected for the foreseeable future and felt perhaps we should not move forward with the expansion of Maupintour and Gutsy Women Travel. He didn't think they would be viable businesses in the aftermath of 9/11.

I took a deep breath and said something along these lines. "Look, I think it's going to be the strong who will survive. And yes, you have to be a little gutsy to travel right now. But with your financial acumen and all the work we've done, I think it could work and we have nothing to lose. If we close down and cease travel opportunities, the terrorists win."

He thought about it, and to his credit and my relief, he agreed to give us a chance, but with a caveat. "We're not going to invest too much money in this."

I was excited to continue to work with Gail on creating the brand. There were a few missteps along the way, but we also made some smart marketing decisions too. The first misstep was deciding that rather than print our fully designed thirty-two-page brochure, we would produce an eight-page pamphlet, the size of an airline ticket, to cut costs. We mailed it out and started receiving calls from women asking, "What is Gutsy Women?" They didn't understand what Gutsy Women Travel was because we cut so much text to fit the much smaller pamphlet that the whole concept and explanation were lost on the reader.

On the smart marketing side, I remember the night I was with Gail in Las Vegas when we came up with the phone number, 866-IM-GUTSY. And most important the tagline, which says it all: "It's Your Life...Live IT!"

Gail is a guru at creating the image of companies. A color scheme is very important, and Gail always looked at primary colors. She really likes the red/orange color on the color wheel, but my favorite color is purple. We decided to combine the two and they became our company colors. Rob Koch was a great creative marketing manager, who created the priceless logo from clip art of a woman jumping off the globe and made our corporate image complete.

A lesson here for entrepreneurs and marketers is the importance of looking at your brand from every angle: your name, your tagline, your phone number, and your color scheme. These are the basics that define what your brand is and how it will appeal to your market segment. It all begins by understanding who your audience is and what you can uniquely offer them.

We understand it's the nature of women to bond. We like to talk, share, and nurture. So, we knew that our brand was going to be about nurturing and getting like-minded women together who would bond on the road even with strangers. But the gutsy aspect of our brand was not about climbing Mount Everest but rather putting yourself on the top of your to-do list and empowering women to do something good for themselves. It's an affirmation: *I'm important and need time for me.* It is similar to the oxygen demonstration given in a plane when the flight attendant is instructing adults to put their oxygen masks on first and then attend to their children. Gutsy Women Travel is the oxygen that women need to resuscitate from their demanding schedules and the many hats they wear.

We officially launched Gutsy Women Travel at an invitation-only afternoon tea for the press at Gail and Carl's midtown Manhattan apartment, perched high above the city and offering expansive views of the city skyline. When the reporters weren't staring out the windows, they were looking at the original paintings by the likes of Monet, Pissarro, and Remington. Gail quickly captured their attention with our exciting news. Marybeth Bond, who now was a consultant for us, spoke about the power of women as purchasers of travel and the largely untapped niche of specialty travel for women.

I talked about how after 9/11 most companies went into retreat. We did the opposite and set about formulating a profitable strategy for the new economic reality. We did a study of how travel companies managed to survive during and after previous wars like Vietnam, Kosovo, and Desert Storm, and we found the best antidote for pessimism was to introduce new products and new services and to offer exemplary customer service.

Gail explained that a gutsy woman might be a businesswoman, a wife, a homemaker, a sister, a daughter, a caregiver, or all these roles. "She often is depended upon heavily by people in her life but never quite makes time for herself. Even superwoman needs to take time for

*April M. Merenda*

a vacation, to renew body, mind, and spirit, and she probably doesn't have time to plan it."

We knew it was going to take time for women to travel again, so our walking tour through the Cotswolds and Bath was scheduled for Spring 2002. But after our tea party launch, Gutsy Women Travel had the travel press buzzing.

# 3

## *On My Own*

The first trip to England was successful, but because women were still hesitant about international travel, we decided to incorporate domestic trips into our 2002 trip calendar, like Charleston and Savannah. I had been to both places, worked with our local guides, and was very involved in what the trips would look like. Gail suggested I go on the trip. "You're good with the women and this will give you a chance to do more research."

The first trip was Charleston to Savannah via Beaufort, and it was on that trip that I first realized we were far more than a travel marketing company promoting travel for women.

At the first hotel we had a welcoming reception and handed out I'm Gutsy buttons that had our website and our toll-free number. The women loved them and were proudly wearing them.

A woman came up to me and shyly asked if she could have two. I told her of course. Take as many as you like and give it to a friend. She said actually she just wanted the two buttons for herself. She had just recovered from a double mastectomy, and I'll always remember her words. "Having two buttons makes me realize how lucky I am."

Then she told me her story. She used to love to travel, but not long after the mastectomy, her husband passed. With no one to join her, she lost her will to travel, which is not uncommon. As we get older, it's not just becoming widows or divorcées, but your friends and even family become empty nesters, retire, and start moving away. This is a dynamic that women face and finding new friends and travel companions is not easy.

It was at that moment I realized we were offering far more than just travel, but a solution to a lot of the issues women were going through. We were empowering them to realize they are not helpless and that being in the company of like-minded women can be freeing too.

A side note about the buttons. In November 2001, I had attended an ASTA (American Society of Travel Advisors) congress in New York City, where the I'm Gutsy buttons were a big hit. I wore mine to a breakfast for Barbara Bush. She pointed to it and said, "I'm gutsy." I told her we were starting a company for women's travel, and she said, "What a great idea!"

As time went on, the business was growing, but we had a few more missteps and mishaps along the way. The biggest mishap was a trip we were planning to Biloxi, Mississippi. We had spent hours with the Biloxi tourism board, and discovered all the great movies filmed there, the excellent cuisine, the history, and the great clothes.

The trip was scheduled for Spring, 2006 and we wanted to go all out promoting it. Carl reluctantly agreed to letting us run a $15,000 ad in *O The Oprah Magazine* for their September 2005 issue. We were so excited.

And then Hurricane Katrina hit that August. The hotel we were going to stay at was gone. There would be no trip. We quickly called the magazine to pull our ad, but it had been printed in August and was already on newsstands. It was a huge financial hit to our fledgling business.

This was not our last effort at advertising, but ultimately, we found that it was word of mouth that worked best. When we did a good job, women would tell hundreds of other women, and often bring a friend on a trip.

It took three years for us to get to our tipping point. The business was growing, but not as fast as Carl wanted it to grow. He had reached a point that he wanted to focus on more profitable businesses, and he started one of the first hedge funds.

It was December 2005 when he made the announcement that he was selling his travel businesses. "What does this mean for us?" I asked, afraid to hear his answer. I had put my heart and soul into Gutsy Women, and I believed in its potential.

It was Gail who jumped in and saved the day. She suggested that

Carl separate Gutsy Women from the sale and give it to me as part of my severance package. I had been working for them over the past six years and had contributed to the success of the travel businesses.

Gail was a force of nature, and Carl agreed. He gave me the Gutsy Women name, the mailing list, and a year's salary for cash flow as part of my severance package. In his straight shooter manner, I remember him saying something along these lines. "You worked hard for us. I want you to experience owning your own company. And when it's your own company and your own money, you may think twice about buying a $15,000 ad." He added that he didn't think the business would make it, but it would be a good experience for me to have.

Carl was a good man, and I learned a lot about business by just being around him. But it was Gail's selflessness that made this happen. Gutsy Women had been her baby too, and her selfless act to turn it over to me is one that I will always be grateful for. It's why I consider Gail one of my angels.

As Gail and I were creating and growing Gusty Women, we always hummed The Bee Gees' song "Stayin' Alive." By the end of 2005, the Gutsy Women Travel adventures began and I often thought of that as our theme song.

# 4

## *Resiliency Takes on New Meaning*

By the end of December 2005, I owned Gutsy Women. I had no staff, but I had the name and the assets including the mailing list, the toll-free number, 866-IMGUTSY, and the URL for GutsyWomen-Travel.com. The best investment I ever made was to use some of the severance money to trademark the name, the logo, the tagline, and the website.

Then I started getting calls out of the blue from travel companies who wanted to partner with me. I liked owning the company. I didn't want partners, but I needed resources. I had learned from Carl to be careful about who you partner with.

I reached out to the owner of Gate 1 Travel, Dani Pipano, at the US-TOA convention in December 2005. He had a very good reputation in the industry. Gate 1 Travel is a major travel operator, and Dani agreed that his reservation center would answer our phone inquiries and his company would operate our tours. In exchange, I would get a residual on each sale through them. But we had two hurdles to face.

The first was that when Carl Icahn turned the business over to me, Gutsy Women had $150,000 on the books for future tours. Carl explained that since he still owned the company when clients had given us deposits for trips, I needed to go back and tell them the company was now being operated by a new owner and offer them refunds. One of the reasons Dani was interested in working with us was that we already had trips on the books. I emailed and called every single client, and the great news is that they all rebooked. What a relief.

The second hurdle was that the *United States Tour Operators Association* (USTOA), a membership organization that requires tour operators to set aside funds to protect consumer deposits and payments, stipulates the tour operator must have at least 51 percent ownership of the company. I took a leap of faith and ended up signing over 51 percent of Gutsy Women to Gate 1 Travel to have USTOA protection. It turned out to be one of the best things I ever did. And like Gail, Dani turned out to be another one of my angels.

Over the four years we worked with Dani, he nurtured the Gutsy Women Travel brand. He adapted his tours to our model: small groups, female licensed tour guides, boutique hotels, no single supplement, and unique experiences that gave women bragging rights. This all worked well until the recession of 2008/2009 took its toll.

On Christmas Eve 2009 I got the unfortunate but understandable news from Dani that Gate 1 needed their staff to focus on their own tours. But he didn't leave us in the lurch. Dani agreed to run ten of our twenty-four tours that had been planned for us, which gave me time to figure out my next step. He also sold back the 51 percent of his shares to me for one dollar. By that time, thanks to his support, I was able to build the Gutsy Women Travel product and clientele. We were now a multimillion-dollar business. I will always be grateful to Dani.

But my next challenge was how was I going to operate Gutsy Women Travel tours? I wasn't certain at that point, but I was determined to forge ahead. For a while I thought I'd do the tours on my own, and just use a booking agent. After all, I knew the business and how the system worked. But then came the Arab Spring in 2011 and I realized how critical it is to have tour operators on the ground.

In January 2011, we had a sold-out tour to Egypt with sixteen women. By then, I was working at my alma mater, St. John's University. (Yes, things do come full circle but more about that story later.) I was utilizing an excellent tour group, South Sinai Travel Group, owned by Antoine Riad who had wonderful guides, but I had promised the group, many of whom had been on other trips with me, that I would join them for the farewell dinner.

I mentioned to the director of the homeland security division of St. John's that I was going to Cairo for the weekend. He informed me that there was a lot of chatter going on in Egypt and warned me not to go. My response? "I'm the president of Gutsy Women Travel. I have sixteen women there. Unless Delta Airlines cancels my flight, I have no option but to go."

We were no sooner in the air when Delta announced that Cairo was in lockdown. Egypt was in the middle of what would become known as the Arab Spring revolution that eventually overthrew the regime of President Mubarak. The minute we landed we were told that the country had a curfew. We were instructed to proceed to the terminal where we would be greeted by security and would receive further information. I sighed and thought, *it is what it is.*

As we disembarked the plane everyone was heading to the terminal. But on the tarmac, I spotted a man in a jeep holding a sign that read April Merenda. I made my way to the jeep, and he said he was with our handling company, South Sinai Travel.

Since he was picking up a VIP, he was allowed to drive on the tarmac. We then proceeded to the place where the visa officer stamps your landing visa, and my luggage was brought there. I paid the fee, got my stamp, and my driver said he'd take me to the Fairmont Hotel at the airport.

I said, "No, no, our hotel is downtown."

He replied, "Not anymore. There was a fire in the hotel lobby, and since the hotel is downtown where the riots and protestors are, we moved your entire group to the Fairmont for safety reasons. It's more money, but we're absorbing the cost. Your group actually just landed from Luxor, but we have to figure out how to get them from the airport to the hotel."

I replied, "You got me here; we should be able to get them."

When I arrived at the front desk to check in, a gentleman who was waiting there introduced himself as Kimo, our tour director. He had just received word that groups, especially Americans, could leave the airport and go to their hotels. The hotel volunteered to send their airport van with Kimo to pick up our group. When he arrived he calmed everyone and explained we had a small van, and they would make a few trips to get everyone to the hotel.

When they got to the hotel, they were shaken up, and with good reason. They were met with machine guns at the airport, told they were in lockdown, and knew their downtown Cairo hotel was on fire. I greeted them when they arrived and told them all their belongings were here, they all had rooms, the bar was open, and drinks were on me. A couple of our clients said they had checked their carry-on luggage at the Cairo Hotel. After the curfew lifted, Kimo made the trip to downtown Cairo on his own, even though it still wasn't safe, and retrieved their bags.

So now we had to make the best of it. That first night we couldn't leave the hotel and the restaurant was closed, but the hotel would deliver food to our guest rooms. We had women on three separate floors, and I assigned one woman on each floor as a monitor. When the waiters delivered the dinners (at Gutsy's expense) they also delivered a bottle of excellent California wine to each group. I had brought three bottles with me from our recent California Dreaming trip, as a gift from California for Antoine Riad. So that night we were able to gather in small groups, in one room with a good meal and an excellent bottle of wine. We were in it together. Antoine was really my angel in Cairo. Although I think I still owe him a case of California wine.

The hotel also had a pool and spa, so the next morning I negotiated a 25 percent discount for our group for spa services. Kimo laughed that every time he showed up at the hotel to give me an update, I was in the spa. I was also in the spa when Antoine came to check on us. Hey, when life gives you lemons, go to the spa.

It was a very fluid situation, with two days of conflicting messages. Hillary Clinton was secretary of state, and the State Department eventually organized what was at that time, the largest evacuation of U.S. citizens in history. There were five thousand American tourists in Cairo. We were told to report to a terminal area at the airport, where nine people from the State Department logged us in. The State Department was paying people with private planes to get everyone out of Cairo and take us to places like Athens, which is where our group went.

It was a long day at the Cairo airport. We were in line for ten hours, and it was eighty degrees. But there were limited food and drink carts, and we remained in good spirits. One of the highlights was seeing broadcaster Brian Williams, who was doing a telecast from the airport. He stopped to ask us how we were doing. We told him that the State Department assured us they would get us out, and we just had to be patient.

Our only difficult moment was when had to say goodbye at the airport to the one Canadian in our group, Lynda, who had to report to the area where her embassy was getting their people out. Fortunately, she arrived home safely too.

When we arrived in Athens, we were met by representatives from the State Department who had hotels for us (although we had to pay for them). They also had sandwiches, soft drinks and cookies for us. They told us that with our airline tickets we could book our trip home with that carrier, at no extra cost. So, we made the best of it. Here's that word again...*resilience*.

Like all of us, I was fatigued but relieved to get home. I had to be back on campus the next day. After all, I was supposed to be gone for only a weekend. When I arrived on campus I felt like a celebrity. Everyone had been worried. I was interviewed by our communications department and was greeted by everyone including our director of the homeland security division, who to his credit never said, *I told you so.*

I got home that night, exhausted, but I was looking forward to my upcoming speaking engagement at the *New York Times* Travel Show that weekend. And then this happened. After all I had dealt with getting us all safely out of Cairo, I fell down a flight of stairs in my house and dislocated my shoulder. I showed up at the travel show, fresh from Cairo with my arm in a sling. I opened my talk with this line. "Let me clear the air. It's safer to be in Cairo than it is in your own house." It got a great laugh.

I learned a lot about myself from that experience. I realized I was stronger than I imagined, I had remained calm throughout, and I kept our group safe. I was a resilient, gutsy woman.

But wait...2011 had more in store for us.

In May, Iceland's Grímsvötn volcano erupted, sending an ash plume twelve miles high. The ash clouds were everywhere and resulted in a six-day flight ban and the cancellation of ninety-five thousand flights, including all of our trips to Europe. Resilience was needed again.

In the lessons learned category, after Cairo I realized you need boots on the ground with a major tour operator, and since then that is how I have worked. Twenty years later, while I still own the company, I outsource the tour operations but ensure they mirror the Gutsy Women signature formula.

Here's a side note. Since we mentioned Hillary Clinton in this chapter, we were flattered when she used our name, Gutsy Women, in her book, *The Book of Gutsy Women: Favorite Stories of Courage and Resilience.* Yep, we've lived it.

# 5

## *It's About the Journey*

When we started Gutsy Women, it was from a business and marketing perspective. Here was an opportunity to tap into the unmet needs of women who wanted to travel on their own, a marketing segment that no one was speaking to. Little did I know that I was embarking on a journey that was far more than just a business venture, but a life-altering experience that would change not only my life, but the lives of so many other women.

My first eye-opening experience was in Savannah on my maiden Gutsy Women trip when I met the woman who wanted two of our I'm Gutsy buttons to remind herself how lucky she was to have survived breast cancer and the loss of her husband. It was in that moment I realized we were offering something much more than travel for women who play many different roles in life. Gail Golden-Icahn always said, "A gutsy woman could be a mother, a daughter, a wife, a caretaker, and I always added, "Or all of those things."

Women live complex and demanding lives, and the last person we usually take care of is ourselves. Travel gives us a chance to do something for ourselves with like-minded women, and whether we are single, divorced, married, or widowed, we find a commonality and a bond in being female. It's a chance to do the things we like to do, to clear our heads, to be ourselves, to be present in the moment, and to put whatever is going on in our lives on pause. We return home feeling restored and energized.

I experienced this just recently on our first Gutsy Women trip to Iceland after the pandemic travel lockdowns. I admit that, like so many people, I was feeling depressed. We have lived through a terrible catastrophe on so many levels. But this trip made me feel hopeful again. It was encouraging to be so well received by the Icelandic people. We were not the ugly Americans, and it was refreshing to be welcomed by a country that had so much to offer us.

It was a joyous occasion to travel again with a wonderful group of women pioneers who were excited to be on their first travel adventure in nearly two years. We had all missed travel, but we had also missed the camaraderie of a shared experience with other women.

On Gutsy Women trips over the years, I have met some incredible women who have not only been transformed by our trips but have become wonderful friends. With their permission, I am sharing a few of their stories and how the Gutsy Women experience changed their lives.

### Meet Gutsy Montez (aka Monty)

Monty is a wife, mother to three sons, and a grandmother. For years she has been a caregiver to her husband who is physically disabled. About a decade ago, she was feeling overwhelmed. A friend suggested that what she needed was a break from it all and told her about Gutsy Women. She contacted me and after chatting about our various upcoming trips, she booked our African safari in 2012.

She had never traveled on her own, but once she booked the trip, she went all in. She took a course in photography and researched what she needed to wear, what she needed to bring, and what she was going to see. Then she started excitedly telling some girlfriends, so a few of them decided to go too. It was an adventure that literally changed her life.

After the trip, she reached out to me to say what a great experience it was and she shared some of her wonderful photos. I hadn't been on that trip, and Monty wanted to know when we could meet each other. I told her I would be on our river cruise through Eastern Europe in 2013, and she booked it. That's when I first met Monty and heard her whole story.

Since that first trip, Monty has been on seventeen of our Gutsy Women tours and is our number one client. We honored her as our Gutsy Woman of the Year at our Sweet Sixteen party in 2017. We put together a video to celebrate her and all the trips she has been on, from the African safari to Morocco, Iceland, and so many more.

These trips have been emotionally, spiritually, and physically transformative. On that first trip, she weighed about three hundred pounds and decided to get healthy. Seventeen trips later, she is about half the size she was then. There were audible gasps at our Sweet Sixteen Party when attendees met the now svelte Monty.

She loves to shop, and on every trip ends up buying an extra suitcase filled with goodies for her sons, daughters-in-law, grandkids, and husband. She and her husband built a farmhouse in South Carolina, and it's proudly decorated with items and mementos from her life's travels.

Sadly, while her husband's health continues to decline, Monty at seventy-two, says she's not afraid because she knows she will have the community of gutsy women for support. On trips over the years, she had met other women who were going through the same things she was. When she would sometimes feel guilty about being on a trip, they said it probably made her husband happy to see her getting a break. These women have each other's backs. The travel and the journey have changed her life.

## Meet Gutsy Larraine

As I was writing this book, I reached out to Larraine who has taken fifteen Gutsy Women trips to ask her if I could include her story. She told me she was recently diagnosed with cancer. We talked and while she was distraught about her illness, she was happy with all she had done at this point in her life. So many people say they'll travel when they retire, or when their kids are grown, or have some other reason to wait for someday. The lesson Larraine wanted to share with everyone is that someday is now. That turned out to be very poignant. She spent her sixty-seventh birthday in the hospital and a week later she passed away.

A widow with one son, she was a caregiver to her mother for many years. With no daughters or sisters, she craved feminine interaction, and found that on the Gutsy Women trips she took over the years.

She was happy she found Gutsy Women and felt blessed to have had the chance to see so many incredible places with other gutsy women. We always said Larraine was like a candy store, and she brought the best snacks like chocolates and cookies to share with everyone on the trip. Everyone loved when she was on their tour.

Of all the guided vacations she took with us, the one that had the most meaning was to our national parks. From Mount Rushmore to Yellowstone and Jackson Hole, she was moved by the majesty of it all in our own backyard, in our beautiful country. It was a trip that felt she had come full circle. We will dearly miss Larraine—she was one gutsy woman.

## Meet Gutsy Tania

Tania, another one of our Iceland pioneers, is married and while she has no children, she has a dog she adores. She lives in Nevada and left a career in pharmaceuticals to take care of her mother who lives in Southern California. Her mother doesn't qualify for any kind of assistance so she and her sister share caregiving. She commutes back and forth to Las Vegas, and at the age of sixty-five it's taken a toll on her.

She found out about Gutsy Women through a friend and takes one trip a year. Her husband says she deserves it. She says it's saved her life. On our trips, she has met many caretakers (including me) who have helped her with the feelings of anger and being sorry for herself. She has found solitude and peace and knows that caregiving is a transition in life that comes to many of us. She now knows that part of handling it well is doing something for herself. The yearly trip gives her the energy she needs and renews her spirits.

## Meet Gutsy Pat with the Hat

When Pat lost her longtime partner, George, in 2007, she was heartbroken. She wanted to get away, and when she heard about Gutsy Women she booked our trip to China, and that's where I met her. Her trip did not start out well. She was flying from JFK to Canada and then on to Hong Kong and China. But she got stuck in Canada and called me in a panic. I calmed her down. She was able to get a flight the next day and I made arrangements for our tour company to pick her up at the airport. The day she arrived our group was going to a park to meet some local artists. I told our guide that I would stay with the group, and she could take Pat on a private tour of the places she had missed the day before, including Tiananmen Square. She was so grateful we did that for her.

That trip changed her life. We did so many special things including dinner with a local women's group, a visit to a private apartment, and a private student dance group who performed traditional dances. It was a down-to-earth trip that helped her ease the pain of losing George. And being with other women who were widows helped her realize she wasn't alone. The trip was therapy for her. It was also the start of a great friendship between us.

Pat is known for her hats. On each trip she wears a different one. Sometimes it's a baseball cap, or a cowboy hat, but we are always entertained with her choice and can't wait to see what's on her head.

Pat continues to travel with us, but one very poignant trip was with her mother. It was called California Dreaming and it was a trip I had personally planned that went from San Francisco and the Napa wineries to Los Angeles ending in Beverly Hills. I immediately clicked with Pat's mom. She was very much like me—a Chico's addict with tags still hanging on clothes, who loved makeup, and was a girly girl. She loved the camaraderie with the group but especially with her daughter and the chance to celebrate life. Three months later she passed away peacefully. Pat and her mother, who never traveled much together, were so glad they had that trip.

In another one of the series of coincidences in this book, or perhaps things that happen by design, Pat's mother, Marie, is buried in Holy Cross Cemetery, twenty feet from my mother's gravesite. When I visit my mother, I always stop by to visit Marie.

## Meet Gutsy Camille

Camille is my baby sister, and always will be no matter how old we are. She is married, has three boys, and is my biggest cheerleader. As a homemaker, wife, and working mom, she had never really traveled much on her own. When my mother, who is from Salerno, Italy, was approaching ninety, we decided to celebrate.

I arranged a Gutsy Women trip in 2009 to the Amalfi Coast and reserved a place for my mother and two of my sisters, Camille and Diana. I organized a pre-trip with a private driver to San Pietro, my mother's hometown. When we arrived, the whole town was there waiting for Gilda. Our family owns a local spot there called Bar Rio. It's a gathering place where the locals meet for espresso, paninis, and the best gelato anywhere. That's where we hung out to meet and greet cousins, aunts, and uncles. It's a trip we will cherish forever.

Camille had an incredible smile the whole time. After that trip she did two other trips, to Montreal and Quebec, and also joined our New York City Holiday Tour, which our mother was also on. Fast-forward to 2021 when she joined the gutsy women pandemic pioneers on the Iceland trip, and I saw that glow and smile again. I think for married women, with all the hats they wear, it's a true testament to how travel brings out the inner glow. I hadn't seen that glow in my sister in a decade.

For Camille, who never did anything for herself, that trip opened her eyes to the one thing she was doing wrong in her marriage and with her children—she was neglecting herself. She came home energized. She also got into walking in Italy, which is something she continued when she returned. She loved trying different cuisines, meeting the other women, and having heartfelt talks about raising children. She realized other women were going through the same things, and it made her feel less alone. The trip changed her life in many ways. It created a better bond with our mother and between us as sisters, along with understanding the roots of our family. It also made her a better wife and mother simply by being a better person to herself.

## Meet Gutsy Pam

Pam was a high-powered executive, now retired at sixty-nine, who went through a difficult divorce. Friends took sides, and as she said, you lose a little bit of your life and yourself. She needed a getaway and booked her first trip on her own with us to Florence and Tuscany. On her next trip to Venice and Lake Como, her sister, who is her closest friend and confidant, joined her. It was a wonderful experience. Their next trip was our Burgundy and Provence river cruise. I met them on that trip.

One of my favorite Gutsy Women photos is of the group, which included Pam and her sister, on a speedboat in the canals of Venice having the most glorious time. They were also treated to a private concert in the town where Pavarotti is from, a cheese extravaganza, and many other special experiences. Pam continues to travel with and without her sister. She was also one of the pandemic pioneers on the Iceland trip.

There is still some hurt from the divorce that she says never really goes away, but you deal with it and move on.

In Iceland she said to the group, "I'm living a dream. Everyone is home, and we're here. What a great opportunity." She's already booked her trip for 2023 to Ireland. She shared her philosophy that if you want things to happen, you have to plan. "I treat myself like I would my job." Wise words.

## Meet Gutsy Chris

Chris was a gutsy woman traveler long before I coined the term as a description for adventures that empower women. She had traveled the world with friends, with family, and on her own. She's trekked over glaciers in Alaska, slept in a tent in the Sahara desert, and roamed the ruins of Angkor Wat in Siem Reap, Cambodia. She spent two months on a freighter going from port to port in South America, weekended in Paris, and capped a visit to Israel with a side trip to Petra, Jordan.

She was used to living on the edge from her career as the TV producer for an iconic advertising agency where she created campaigns and videos for, among many others, Reebok, MTV, and Bob Dylan. Fifteen years ago, after shepherding her mother through her final illness, she embarked on a new journey. She returned to school for a master's in social work, and since then has devoted herself to serving older adults.

Now, on the eve of starting treatments for her own illness—a non-aggressive form of non-Hodgkin's lymphoma—Chris was looking for a trip that combined adventure travel with pampering herself. One of her daughters—twenty-one-year-old Fei Fei, herself a world traveler—would join her. My Iceland trip seemed perfect for them.

It didn't get off to the best start when Chris and Fei Fei failed to meet us in the Delta Club Lounge at Kennedy Airport before the flight. There was confusion about the tickets, and they were booked for the next day. Mix-ups like this don't put a damper on gutsy women, and they joined us a day later. I was able to rush their COVID tests so they could be with the group for Retreat Spa Blue Lagoon. So, it turned out that all they missed was a day of quarantine in the hotel. After the stress of the airline misadventure, the luxurious Blue Lagoon treatment was especially welcome and rejuvenating. Chris's resilience was on full display at the end of the day when she rose at dinner to toast all of us gutsy women, saying "Isn't it great that we're all here together!"

It was a grand beginning to a wonderful Iceland experience of nat-

*April M. Merenda*

ural beauty, spectacular hikes, luxury treatment, warm social inter-actions, and great fun. Chris is an independent spirit and before this trip, she had been unsure about traveling in a group. I persuaded her that you don't lose your individuality in our band of merry gutsy women; you enjoy the company of other fascinating individuals. It clearly worked; Chris has already signed up for our next trip to Greece in May of 2022.

## Meet Gutsy Dorinda

In 2001 Dorinda's mother passed away suddenly and she made ar-rangements to have her service on September 15, 2001. This was within days of the 9/11 tragedy and grief was already visiting, but its presence enlarged exponentially!

She decided travel would help with her grief. She heard about Gutsy Women Travel and reviewed the available trips. She signed up for the New York Holiday tour and has always proclaimed it was one of the best things she did for herself. Over the next few years, she joined other Gutsy Women Travel tours to China, Peru, Quebec, and Egypt, always traveling as a single.

When she registered for our Quebec trip, I emailed her that anoth-er woman, Carol from Los Angeles, would be joining the trip. Both Dorinda and Carol had to fly to Canada the day before the start of the tour. Prior to leaving they emailed each other and agreed to have din-ner upon arrival. They really enjoyed the tour that included me, my mother, Gilda, and my sister Camille as part of the overall group, and at the end of the tour they agreed to stay in touch.

They discovered they lived only about thirty minutes apart in Cal-ifornia. As a retiree from Kaiser Permanente, Dorinda was asked to work on a temp project, and Carol's business was located nearby. She and Carol would often meet for lunch and also enjoyed many day trips that L.A. offers.

In January 2011, Dorinda and Carol left to see the wonders of Egypt with Gutsy Women. Ten days into our tour, flying back to Cairo from Abu Simbel, the January 25 revolution erupted. They landed to a locked down airport and had no idea what was happening. It was Car-ol's birthday, and they somehow managed to get some hamburgers from Burger King, thinking they would probably be sleeping at the airport.

Luckily, I had landed in Cairo that same day, and miraculously arranged for the hotel van to take Dorinda, Carol, and the other fourteen women in the group to our hotel now near the airport. And so the lockdown and curfew experience began.

Room service was arranged, and Carol and Dorinda watched the events on CNN. It appeared we would be here for a while, so they arranged for massages the next day. A concerned friend called the hotel asking for Dorinda and Carol. Staffing was scarce and whoever answered her call told her "Oh! They are having a massage and a beer." They still giggle at this memory!

On the third day, the State Department commandeered a VIP terminal for evacuation, and we were transferred to the Cairo airport. We stood for over ten hours, with limited food and little access to water. There was only one bathroom for thousands of people!

Finally, Carol and Dorinda got the last two seats to Athens. That's when they noticed that painted on the side of the plane were balloons and the name Small Planet Airways, a Lithuanian company. The plane was full and that's when they saw the cabin crew. They were dressed in camel-colored sheath dresses, with three-inch-wide orange patent leather belts and camel pillbox hats–so 70s. Dorinda thought she was hallucinating.

Fortunately, the flight to Athens was uneventful. They were met at the staircase by the U.S. ambassador to Egypt. The State Department was terrific and handled passport control, their bags, and arranged for rooms at a hotel at the airport. They even kept the kitchen open so they could eat.

The next morning, they flew to Paris for a night, and the following day they left Paris in the snow wearing their clothes for the desert.

Having experienced the turmoil of the trip together, Carol and Dorinda became forever friends. Up until COVID, they have traveled somewhere every month.

Dorinda says travel has enriched her mind and soul. She is so grateful that she discovered Gutsy Women Travel. The first trip to New York helped her out of a very dark period, and it encouraged her to continue to see our beautiful world.

## Meet Gutsy April

As I was writing about how the Gutsy Women experience changed the lives of the women above, I realized there was more to my story too.

I always felt that my lot in life was different than my three sisters, and many other women I know as well. I never married or had children, but I don't regret it. I don't feel it was a necessity to having a fulfilling life. If the opportunity for a forever partner had happened, that would have been great. But I've known some wonderful men, had great relationships, and I've experienced love.

The real love of my life was George. I met him when I moved to California in 1982, and I bought a car from his dealership. We became best friends first and then became a couple. While we maintained separate residences, we were together for seventeen years, but we never quite progressed to marriage. In 1999 when I told George about the job opportunity in Kansas, I was hoping this would put our relationship in perspective for him and he would ask me to stay, which I would have. Instead, he threw me a going-away party.

Fast-forward to 2019. I got an email from George's wife, sharing with me that George had passed away. He wanted her to let me know that I had been the love of his life (something he had told her even before they married). He wanted me to know when he let me go to Kansas without asking me to stay, it's because he didn't want to stand in the way of such a great career opportunity. It was a mind boggling revelation.

I never had children because I was always realistic, and I didn't think my traveling career and lifestyle was a foundation to grow a family. But I am a nurturer and I've invested that quality with my nieces and nephews, my students, my clients, and as a caregiver to my mother.

On nearly all our trips there is a woman who is a caregiver, often for their mother. It's a common experience for many boomer women. I frequently have conversations with them and let them know it's okay to feel angry and frustrated sometimes, but it's not okay to let their mother see that. I felt it was the greatest honor of my life to care for the woman who gave birth to me. But it's also important for caretakers to take care of themselves too, and a trip can be a magical elixir.

I've learned a lot about resilience. I've also kept reinventing myself. I never thought that when I graduated from college, I would have a career in travel or academia where traditionally you need a PhD. I was afforded that opportunity because of my industry experience, which is an asset in higher education. I have grown and developed because of Gutsy Women, which made me a better person, a better professor, and a better business owner.

But the biggest lesson I have learned is that our Gutsy tagline, *It's Your Life...Live IT!* is much more than a tagline. It's a philosophy of my life. It's your life, with the emphasis on *your*. You are responsible for *your life,* and you should live it as you want to. I try to share that philosophy with everyone I meet. When they get it, I've done my job.

# 6

## *Where's Melissa?*

When I travel with our groups, I often tell the story of Melissa. Not only is it a great story that shows how resilient and resourceful women are, but it's a great travel lesson too.

One morning on one of our earliest trips to Paris and the Loire Valley, our group toured the Louvre. One of our tour members was Melissa, for whom visiting the Louvre was a lifelong dream. She had bought several prints to decorate her home. Other women had bought souvenirs and were excitedly discussing their purchases as we got on our bus to head back to our hotel. We were on the Champs-Élysées when our tour director said we were approaching the best macaron bakery in all of Paris, Ladurée, and she wanted to treat us to this experience. The bus driver agreed to make a stop, but we had to return to the bus quickly because he wasn't really allowed to park there.

We left our things on the bus and went into this famous bakery. Right next to the bakery was a newsstand with all the gossipy celebrity tabloid magazines. As we were eating our delicious macarons some of us wandered over there to take a look, including Melissa. The tour director came over and told us we had to quickly get back on our bus. We were excited about getting ready for our cooking lesson that evening at the world-renowned École Ritz Escoffier at the Ritz Hotel.

As we boarded, the driver quickly did a head count and I settled into the back of the bus. We arrived at our hotel and as I was making my way to the front, I noticed a seat with items on it. It had several prints from the Louvre, a purse, and other items including a cell phone. That's when it hit me! I shouted to our tour guide, *"Oh my God, where's Melissa?"* She replied that the driver had done a head count and I replied, "Well, obviously incorrectly!" By then we were about two miles from the newsstand, the traffic was heavy, and the driver said it would be like looking for the proverbial needle in a haystack. I was in panic mode.

Meanwhile, Melissa was now stuck in the middle of the Champs-Élysées without her purse or her cell phone. We had just landed the day before and for the life of her, she could not remember the name of our hotel. But she did remember that the cooking school was at the Ritz. She stopped a policeman and asked him how to get there.

It was a bit of a walk, but she found her way there. She went to the concierge and embarrassingly told him her plight, and that the group was coming there to École Ritz Escoffier that night. He sent her to the cooking school on the lower floor and thank goodness they had the name of the hotel we were staying in, which happened to be George V. See how easy it is to forget even the simplest of names?

I love to tell this story because it shows how resilient and resourceful women are. Melissa didn't panic, and figured out how to find us.

There's also a major travel lesson here. Always make certain to have the names and phone numbers of the hotels you are staying in with you. It's very easy to forget. Not that it would have helped Melissa, since she didn't have her purse, but it helped me on our first trip to Iceland after the pandemic. (More about that further in the book.) I had to go to the hospital in an ambulance with one of our women who fell ill, and fortunately I had asked for the business card of the farmhouse we were staying in. That came in very handy when the hospital needed the address and we needed to get back.

Here's another travel lesson. Fast forward to our Memphis and Nashville tour in October 2021. Our top client Monty (who you read about in Chapter 5) packed her custom-made cowboy boots and realized when the group arrived in Nashville that she had left them in the closet in the Memphis hotel room. While the hotel shipped them back to her home, she regretted not having them for the private line dancing lesson at the Whitehorse Saloon in downtown Nashville. Those boots join the countless items our clients have left behind over our twenty years of operation. Heed our advice and always double check your closet and drawers before checking out.

Not every story from the road is as dramatic as Melissa's and Monty's, but there are many that are heartwarming, poignant, and inspiring. Here are a few of my favorites.

## Two Strangers Become Best Friends

Debra and Angie (one is from the U.S. and the other is from Canada) did not know each other when they separately booked our 2010 trip to Tuscany. It was Debra's first adventure by herself. When her long-time travel buddy could no longer travel, she looked up *solo women travel*, and Gutsy Women came up. She loved the name. Her daughter was concerned that she was traveling with people she had never met. It was on the Tuscany trip that she met Angie and they have become treasured friends. They travel together every year, and their last trip was to Venice in 2019. They're looking forward to traveling again soon.

## Twin Sisters and a Poignant Trip

Donna has traveled all her life and is a connector with friends everywhere. When her husband was diagnosed with cancer and couldn't travel as much, he encouraged her to continue to take trips. She found trips that didn't take her away for too long and made new connections with Gutsy Women. Her husband felt good that she was in a safe environment and was not alone.

When she went on our Costa Rica trip in 2014, she said, "I've got to get my twin sister Sharry on a trip." But as often happens in our busy lives, they kept putting it off. Then her sister was diagnosed with cancer. With their seventieth birthdays coming up, they decided to celebrate with a trip to Iceland. At the encouragement of her doctors, her sister took the trip. They had a wonderful time and shortly after, her sister passed away. Donna is grateful to have these memories and we have a beautiful photo in our photo gallery of the sisters blowing out their candles, on their last trip together.

Just recently, Donna's husband passed away, and she's grateful that the Gutsy Women community is here for her after losing both her sister and her husband. She knows that she has a wealth of friends and a community that will support her. She's planning her next trip.

## Meet the "Italian Princesses"

In 2007, Sandra and Maria booked our tour to the Amalfi Coast. In a rare occurrence, the other women who signed up for the trip were not able to go. It was a family group of women—the mother, daughter, and granddaughters. Just before the trip the mother fell and broke her hip, and they all canceled. We didn't want to cancel the tour, so Sandra and Maria had an incredible private tour that we now call the "Princess Tour." Every morning they were picked up in a Mercedes with a private driver to take them on the day's explorations with just the two of them.

They ended up becoming besties and have since traveled together almost every single year. They have taken twelve trips together including five Gutsy Women trips to Amalfi, Budapest/Prague, Provence, Tuscany, and Greece. Every trip has been an amazing experience with great memories. They love that Gutsy Women brought them together.

## Leave the Details to Us

Joan is single and a high-powered Realtor in Florida. She has a demanding and all-consuming career she loves, in addition to nurturing her family circle. She's a take-charge, take-control powerhouse, but every year she enjoys the comfort of a Gutsy Women trip and letting us handle all the details.

It started with her first trip on one of our safaris over a decade ago. She met several other women on that trip who all clicked, and at the end of the safari they said to each other, "Where are we going next?" Since then, Joan has been to Panama, Iceland, Ireland, and our European River Cruise. She has already booked our Greece trip for May 2022, which is now sold out.

Joan is a perfectionist, but she doesn't have time to research and handle all the details of a trip. Even though we are not always perfect, we have never let her down and she has remained a loyal client.

Joan had one bad experience when she booked a Danube River cruise. Because she is so busy, she hadn't realized that it wasn't a Gutsy Women-only group, and much to her surprise she was the only gutsy woman on the cruise along with mostly couples. She ended up having a great time and sent me wonderful photos from the trip, but she felt we had not been transparent. I took that to heart. I always want our clients to be happy and I value loyalty, so her next trip was on us. She was in awe of that resolution and what we did for her.

For Joan, Gutsy Women is one-stop shopping. She knows we'll take care of everything and she can just relax and enjoy the trip.

## Getting Away from It All

Valerie lives in California and has a very full and busy life. She's married, has a family, and owns a business, but once a year she takes a trip on her own. It's her self-care trip and a chance to clear her head and regroup.

She's been traveling with us for a decade. On one of our trips, she met a couple of women who all enjoyed each other's company and they decided to book another trip together. But Valerie has no problem going by herself and has already made plans to go on our Spain and Portugal trip on her own. She always returns home renewed by her annual getaway.

Whether you travel solo, or with friends and family, and whether you're single, married, widowed, or divorced—whatever your reasons for getting away are—there is one thing you have in common with other gutsy women: you never know where the road will take you.

*April M. Merenda*

# Photo Gallery

*Gutsy Women Logo*

*Gail Golden-Icahn and April, GWT 10th Anniversary celebration*

*Amalfi Coast April and Gabriella*

*Amalfi Coast Dinner in Sorrento with Gilda and sisters Diana and Camille*

*April M. Merenda*

*Amalfi Coast Gilda taking charge at the Sorrento Cooking School with Camille*

*Amalfi Coast Annette at the Sorrento Cooking class*

*Angel Antonie Riad with Gutsy Women in Cairo*

*Angel Dean Kathleen Voute MacDonald with my nephew Jonathan*

*April M. Merenda*

*Angel Gail Golden-Icahn (right) greeting past traveler Margaret*

*April with her brother, sisters, and Gilda*

*April & familia*

*April at Stonehenge*

*April M. Merenda*

*April at the NY Times Travel Show Meet the Experts*

*April moderating a panel at the NY Times Travel Show*

*April in Glasgow*

*Gusty Women launch, November 2001*

*April M. Merenda*

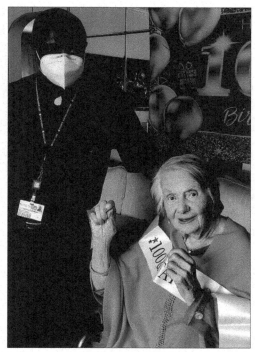

*Gilda Merenda faux 100th birthday party with Rev Fr Kyrian*

*Gutsy 16th Celebration*

*Gutsy 16th Celebration*

*Gutsy 16th Celebration*

*April M. Merenda*

*Gutsy 16th Celebration*

*Gutsy 16th Celebration*

*Gutsy 16th with my SJU angels*

*Gutsy Anne and Danielle in Cabo*

*Gutsy Dorinda and Carol in Quebec cooking class*

*Gutsy Camille*

*Gutsy Donna and her twin sister Sharry in Iceland*

*Gutsy Donna and her twin sister Sharry celebrating their milestone birthday in Iceland*

*April M. Merenda*

*Gutsy Joan enjoying her river cruise*

*Gutsy Lynda and Gutsy Valerie*

*Gutsy Montez in Havana Cuba*

*Gutsy Montez on the National Parks trip*

*April M. Merenda*

*Gutsy Montez, April and Larraine in Costa Rica NYE 2019*

*Photo from Gutsy Women Safari*

*Gutsy Sandy and Lisa in India*

*Gutsy Tania (right) gifting April with a Gutsy Women pendant in Cabo*

*April M. Merenda*

*Pandemic Travel; Gutsy Women at Graceland Memphis TN*

*Gutsy Women celebration at the Benjamin Hotel NYC*

It's Your Life...Live IT!

*Gutsy Women Cooking Class Rome, Italy*

*Gutsy Women go shopping at Harrods*

*April M. Merenda*

*Gutsy Women in the Hamptons*

*Gutsy Women in Australia*

*Gutsy Women in China*

*Gutsy Women in Costa Rica*

*April M. Merenda*

*Gutsy Women in Costa Rica doing Yoga*

*Gutsy Women in Costa Rica hot spring*

*Gutsy Women in Ireland*

*Gutsy Women in NYC*

*April M. Merenda*

*Gutsy Women in Japan*

*Gutsy Kate and her sister Eileen touring the Czech Republic*

*Gutsy Women in the United Kingdom*

*Home visit in Wales*

*April M. Merenda*

*I'm Gutsy Button*

*Chris, Fei Fei, and my sister Camille in Iceland*

*Gutsy Caroline at active volcano in Iceland*

*Iceland Red Hair!*

*April M. Merenda*

*Iceland van with step stool!*

*Iceland Waterfalls*

*April and the NY Pioneers viewing the Iceland Glaciers*

*April following Rainbows and Waterfalls in Iceland*

*April M. Merenda*

*Gutsy Chris and Gutsy April in Iceland*

*Gutsy Pam enjoying the many waterfalls in Iceland*

*Gutsy Pioneers ferrying through the glaciers in Iceland*

*Gutsy Women Pioneers visiting the active volcano site in Reykjavik*

*April M. Merenda*

*Icelandic Horses*

*Icelandic Horse*

*Icelandic Last Night in Reykjavik*

*Retreat Spa Blue Lagoon*

*April M. Merenda*

*Retreat Spa Blue Lagoon Iceland*

*Retreat Spa Blue Lagoon Iceland*

*Retreat Spa Blue Lagoon*

*Reyka Vodka & Icelandic Shark*

*April M. Merenda*

*The Gutsy women pioneers in Westman Island, Iceland*

*The pandemic pioneers in Iceland*

*Icelandic Women Spinning*

*Gutsy April with Noury in Morocco*

*April M. Merenda*

*Gutsy women in Morocco*

*Gutsy women in the Sahara*

*Gutsy April in Morocco*

*Gutsy Pam with her sister in Venice on their way to Murano, Italy*

*April M. Merenda*

*Pat with the Hat viewing the geysers on the National Parks trip*

*Peru local women in The Scared Valley*

*April with Peruvian school children*

*Gutsy Caryn and the Sacred Valley*

*April M. Merenda*

*Gutsy Barb in Peru*

*Jodie, April and Pat with the Hat exploring Machu Picchu*

*SJU April at CCPS Faculty Convocation*

*SJU Basketball Team has been a big part of our legacy*

*April M. Merenda*

*SJU BFF alumna Sue Wilson, Mary Helmlinger and Chris Crowley*

*Professor Merenda and her students at Conrad Hilton NY*

*SJU Hospitality students at the Parco Di Principi Hotel in Rome with Professor Merenda*

*SJU Professor Merenda and her students at the SJU Rome campus*

*April M. Merenda*

*SJU Professor Merenda with MSIHM Students*

*Gutsy Women pandemic pioneers in Iceland*

*The picture of the Gutsy Women pandemic pioneers in Iceland that went viral*

# 7

## Top Destinations for Gutsy Women

In twenty years of creating memorable travel experiences for women, we've learned a lot about what women want, and their favorite destinations. We believe that there is a gutsy woman inside each of us. Over the years Gutsy Women Travel has developed a community of women who have experienced amazing adventures.

From the very first trip in 2002, our goal was to provide women with the chance to recharge their energies and travel is one of the best ways to do just that! We have always focused on travel experiences tailored to what women want. That includes a great, secure hotel location, quality and comfort in accommodations, trip pacing (guests generally stay at least two days in any given hotel), unique experiences they couldn't do on their own, and the opportunity to meet local people, plus free time for individual exploration. We do this in the comfort of a small group (on average ten to sixteen women) while offering value and attractive price points.

Our trips have spanned the globe from Antarctica to Asia and just about every other continent in between, but there are ten places that consistently make our top ten places women want to visit.

### 1. Italy, Italy, Italy

Women cannot get enough of this country. I truly believe all women are Italophiles in disguise! The traditional Rome, Florence, and Venice tour has been featured over the years as well as combinations of Venice and Lake Cuomo or Florence and Montecatini and, of course,

Sicily. But by far the biggest draw has been the Amalfi Coast. I do not say this because my roots are from Italy but as an authority on what and where women want to go, and hands down it's the Amalfi Coast.

At Gutsy Women Travel we like to include a pre-night in Rome to gather the travelers who come from all over the U.S.A. and different parts of world to join our trips and get acclimated. We then proceed to the Amalfi Coast, stop at Pompeii on the way, and usually have a luncheon near the lemon groves for our first taste of limoncello before continuing on.

We have featured stay put packages in Sorrento where women do day trips and do not have to pack and unpack every day. Must-see stops include Positano, Capri, Ravello, and the Magna Graecia region where we visit an agricultural farm where ricotta and mozzarella are made.

By far, of the thousands of women over the past twenty years who experienced our guided vacations, Italy is numero uno!

My number one tip in Italy, and an absolute must, is to do a hands-on cooking class. They are offered in every major city including Rome, Florence, Venice, Milan, and Bologna. On our Amalfi trip with my mother and sisters, we went to the Sorrento Cooking School. It's very high-end but there are others that are less expensive like Eataly's cooking classes. It's a wonderful and fun experience to cook with others and a great way to discover the flavor and cuisine of the destination.

## 2. France

A close second to Italy are our trips to France. There are so many areas to visit so women can book year after year and never tire of this destination. Paris and Loire Valley has been very popular as well as our Burgundy and Provence River Cruise or Paris and Normandy combination. I had the opportunity to join our trip to Normandy for the seventieth anniversary of D-Day. I strongly suggest every woman should take the opportunity to go there. It is very moving, and it will make you appreciate even more the sacrifices made by the greatest generation in World War II.

My top tip for Paris is to go there for Bastille Day, which is their national holiday. Over two days, the French celebrate with free entertainment, a military parade, outdoor concerts, and spectacular fireworks. The Eiffel Tower becomes a magical sound and light show. And it's a great time to shop. The shops have fabulous sales and discounts.

## 3. Peru

Peru is a magical, mystical, and spiritual destination that seems to affect women deep down more than most other countries. Maybe it's the history, the people, their customs...but anyone who has traveled there has said it touched their inner being.

I spent my fifty-fifth birthday in Peru. I had a shaman ceremony in the Sacred Valley and it was truly amazing. It's an experience I recommend to anyone going there. It's poignant and mystical, and an important part of the culture of Peru. If you have not been there, add it to your bucket list.

## 4. Morocco

The medina, souks, and overall countryside are magnificent and make it a favorite destination for gutsy women. We have operated Morocco every year since our inception with the exception of 2020 and 2021 due to COVID-19. The women love it and I must say our groups help the economy with the pottery dishware, rugs, leather jackets, scarfs, and beauty products you can purchase and ship home.

I highly recommend that any visit to Morocco should include an overnight stay in the Sahara desert. It is one of the greatest experiences I've ever had, sleeping in a luxury tent, with five-star accommodations and the magnificent night sky above you. The whole Sahara experience is simply breathtaking.

## 5. Costa Rica

Women just love Costa Rica because there is no language barrier, and it is readily accessible by most carriers. It's a trip you can do within a week and come back energized. I have been on our Costa Rica tour three times and each visit intrigued me.

One thing every woman who goes there should experience is river rafting. It's exhilarating, it's safe, and it's a great way to get out of your comfort zone. Zip-lining is another exciting thing to try. But whether its river rafting or zip-lining it will make you feel invincible, and that's something every gutsy woman should experience.

## 6. New York, New York

It's a wonderful town. Women love going to New York and our holiday trip is always a sellout. We feature visits to MoMA, the Metropolitan Museum of Art, the Radio City Christmas Spectacular, and a Broadway show where women go backstage and have a meet and greet with the cast.

There's nothing better than the holiday season in New York, but my top go-to attraction anytime is Central Park. Go for a walk or even spend a day walking the different pathways. You can take a guided tour and learn about the history of how the park was formulated. Many local New Yorkers would benefit from a guided tour to learn about its history and the depth of the park. It's a monumental attraction.

New York is definitely a destination women never tire of.

## 7. Iceland

I finally got to go to Iceland this past year and now I know why it sells out every year we offered it. It's an absolutely breathtaking country. The geothermal waters, waterfalls, and northern lights make it a destination we can offer two times a year.

Iceland was our first Gutsy Women Travel pandemic trip, which I describe in detail later in this book. But of all the different places I've experienced, Retreat Spa Blue Lagoon is by far one of the top experiences of my life. I recommend it to anyone going to Iceland. It will be a treat of a lifetime.

## 8. Japan

Japan sells out every time we offer it. It exudes warmth, customs, tradition, cuisine, art and photography, and so much more. The Japanese people are kind, soft-spoken, and polite. And it is one of the cleanest countries you will ever visit.

From the sights, sounds, and crowds of Tokyo to the sacred palaces of Kyoto, you will find shrines, temples, gardens, zoos, the bamboo forest, traditional tea houses, and then of course more palaces usually perched high on a hill. The Golden Palace (Kinkaku-ji) is breathtaking. On a more somber note, there is an educational museum park in Hiroshima. A special thrill is seeing Mount Fuji from the little train with its wooden floor and couches. It's a great place to experience a very different culture and cuisine.

## 9. Spain/Portugal

Women like to do these countries together or on separate occasions, but they love them both. The history, cultures, cuisine, people, music, and weather make it a woman's dream tour.

Spain and Portugal are two of my specialties. I spent five years selling tours there. One of my favorite places is the Alhambra palace in Granada. It's a UNESCO World Heritage Site and its history and beauty make it one of Spain's major attractions. It was the palace and fortress of the Moorish monarchs and is rich in centuries of history, artwork, gardens, and Islamic architecture.

## 10. South and East Africa

Women love the excitement of a safari, which is truly an adventure of a lifetime. The opportunity to enjoy wildlife, to see the big five up close and personal in their natural habitat, and to learn from the local people will create unforgettable memories. You will want to bring a good high-powered lens camera. Some of the photos taken by women on these trips are extraordinary. A safari is a spiritual and photographic adventure you will cherish forever.

Yes, as Louis Armstrong so beautifully sang, "It's a wonderful world."

# 8

## *And Then the World Stopped*

In November of 2019, I hosted a reception at The Benjamin in Manhattan to launch an exciting Gutsy Women partnership with our new operator. Filled with optimism as we ushered in a new decade, I was looking forward to another wonderful travel year with returning clients and new ones. And then the world stopped.

Very early in the new year, I began to hear rumblings about a virus in China called COVID. It didn't register as something to be concerned about, or maybe I was in denial. That was about to change.

By now, I was also an assistant professor/industry professional in the hospitality management program at St. John's University. I had organized a trip for late February (during spring break) to the Amalfi Coast in Italy for sixteen hospitality students who were in my resort management class. I established a scholarship fund for our hospitality students to help them travel on spring break and experience a destination as part of their learning. The scholarships pay for their airfare, and they just pay for the land trip, which helps make the trip affordable.

I had put the trip together with Perillo Tours and it was going to be fabulous. We would start in Rome and then head down the Amalfi Coast. Each property that we were staying in or visiting was part of the class. We were booked in various resorts up and down the Amalfi Coast. It was going to be a great adventure and learning experience for the students.

In mid-February I got the call from Perillo saying that their intelligence in Rome was reporting that the virus was bad. We were scheduled to fly into Rome on British Airways on February 28. The students were so excited, and I remember thinking, *this can't be happening.*

At around the same time, St. John's University got involved. We have a campus in Rome, and they were alerted from the ministry in Italy that the virus was becoming rampant. While the Amalfi Coast itself wasn't an issue yet, Rome was, and that's where we had to fly in and out of. Based on their intelligence from Italy, which had not yet surfaced here in the States, the university made the decision to shut down all the spring break trips.

The airline did not offer us refunds, but Perillo graciously offered the students credit for a future trip. Then St. John's refunded the money the students had paid for the land trip. Because the scholarship for the airfare was from me, they fortunately weren't out any money. At the time I thought everybody was embellishing what was going on and perhaps overreacting.

It didn't take long before I knew how wrong I was. The outbreaks of COVID-19 had started in Northern Italy in February and spread rapidly. By March 21, all of Italy was in lockdown. At the peak of the pandemic, Italy had the highest number of COVID cases in the world and the highest number of deaths in 2020 since 1945 when Italy was fighting World War II.

By March 1, the airlines were canceling all their flights to Europe and other regions. By mid-March the U.S. was in lockdown. If we had taken our scheduled flight, we would have been stuck in Italy. On March 7, the university closed, and we went to remote learning.

While my academic life had dramatically changed, tourism and Gutsy Women Travel was about to as well. In the beginning, I think everyone was in denial. It wasn't until the airlines stopped flying and we went into lockdown mode that we realized how serious this was.

During the first week of March, I had a conference call with the company operating the Gutsy Women trips. Every tour operator was in unchartered waters, and no one really knew what to do. We had upcoming trips booked and paid for. Our first trip in 2020, which ended up being our only trip, was to Costa Rica over the president's holiday. Our next trip was scheduled to Morocco in March. Some of the women who had booked that trip decided to do a pre-trip, and were already there when the airlines announced they would stop flying. Luckily, they were able to get back.

After talking it through with our operator, we felt that at the end of the day, client safety was the most important thing. There were many tour companies that waited for their clients to cancel the trips. We felt the right thing to do was to preempt the issue by letting our clients know we were canceling our scheduled trips through the end of May, which included the Amalfi Coast, Greece, and Morocco. After the experience with the women who went to Morocco earlier, we didn't want to risk women doing pre-trips and getting stuck overseas.

We made the difficult decision to cancel all our trips through the end of May, thinking that everything would be fine by then. We gave our clients a credit for a future trip. In some circumstances, we refunded their money. We continued to take bookings, however, in good faith, for trips after May.

Well, we all know what happened to travel in 2020. Nothing operated in 2020—nothing. It was a big disappointment, but that was overshadowed by the dynamics of what was happening. A lot of people early on just didn't understand the enormity of the situation.

In Italy, thousands of people were dying, but many did not see the storm coming our way. When I think about the gutsy women who are our client base, I always talk about resiliency, and I felt fortunate that these women understood why we took the steps we did in canceling our trips.

Our industry partners met often with the Trump administration. We were kept informed on what was going on, and they didn't sugarcoat it. They said this was really serious. While we were still taking bookings for later in 2020, we were straightforward and told the women we weren't confident that these trips would happen. As it turned out, everything did come to a standstill.

The decade had started on such a promising note. I was excited about our new Gutsy Women partnership. We had some great trips planned as well as various new programs. It was disappointing and depressing to have everything come to a halt. We also knew everyone was experiencing these emotions, and we knew it was important to keep our Gutsy Women community connected. So, we kept our emails flowing, and turned our messages into helpful hints, connecting women who've been on our trips, and sharing stories. We wanted to keep our Gutsy Women in the family loop. We didn't know what was going to happen in 2020 so we started to focus more on 2021.

There were other parts of the travel industry that were impacted early on too including the major situation with the cruise lines. In March of 2020, I was asked to host a webinar for donors and alumni at St. John's University on what was happening with travel, what was safe, and what wasn't, starting with the cruise lines. Carnival Cruise had people who had died on ships. There were cruise ships off the shores of Miami and L.A. that weren't being allowed to dock.

I was able to get firsthand information from the Cruise Lines International Association (CLIA). In those early days, they believed the virus was spreading through metal contact. Metal on a ship is everywhere—in the gym, on the ship, the handrails, and all the common spaces. The cruise line industry saw the enormity of it, so along with the airlines shutting down, the cruise lines shut down.

Then we had the local situation in New York City. The subways were thought to be one of the biggest sources of spreading the virus, coupled with the density of New York where people are living on top of each other. So, we saw an exodus of people leaving Manhattan to go to the Hamptons, upstate New York, Florida, and New England.

This was happening in big cities across the country. The entire state of California completely shut down. Businesses were closing, and people were working remotely. The experts were learning about this virus in real time so information on how the virus was transmitted was often confusing.

Everything had spiraled downward, and by the summer of 2020 we realized the magnitude of the situation. This was something much bigger than anyone could ever have anticipated.

Realizing the pandemic wasn't going away anytime soon, the question became: How are we going to deal with this? Those of us in the travel industry and academia started being briefed by the medical profession and being apprised of the work on vaccinations. It also became clear that people who were formidable in the industry needed to be leaders.

I like to think that Gutsy Women was a leader. Instead of focusing on short-term profits, we started to think long-term. We stopped taking bookings and focused on developing our trips for 2021. As it turned out, even those were delayed until June of 2021 when Gutsy Women pandemic pioneers went to Iceland. The two-week lockdown that started in March of 2020 turned into an eighteen-month lockdown for travel.

While the travel industry has certainly taken a major hit, subsidies to the airline and cruise industries has helped keep them afloat. The Paycheck Protection Program (PPP) that helped companies pay their employees kept many tour companies alive.

The travel and hospitality businesses that have suffered the most, especially in New York City, have been the food and beverage industry and hotels. Fifty percent of restaurant owners closed their doors, due to high rents they couldn't pay, and they'll never reopen.

As for some of the major hotels in New York that closed, some of them are now going the route of the Plaza and the Waldorf Astoria and becoming condominiums. I think that's a brilliant move.

Of course, all aspects of our lives have changed. Employees started to work from home, and employers found that productivity didn't suffer. For the most part, employees found that working remotely was less stressful and saved them the time and expense of commuting too. I don't think work from home is going to be something that goes away anytime soon.

And in academia, we're finding that although we've enabled students to come to class in person, many have to take online classes because they are not vaccinated. It's another issue that's not going away anytime soon, but by offering a remote option, they can continue their education.

Without sounding too Pollyanna, there is a bright side. The pandemic brought the human spirit together. It made us appreciate our family and friends more than ever. Families spent more time together and enjoyed meals together at home, something that didn't happen often in their busy lives before COVID. Even though we had to social distance and grew weary of contracting the virus, I think the nuclear family and friendships became stronger.

The real isolation came with people living alone, who didn't have the camaraderie of other people. It was especially difficult for seniors. I have said time and again that my mother did not die from COVID, but she died because of COVID. She was so isolated during her time in home hospice. People were nervous to visit for fear of spreading anything to her because of her age. I often wonder, had there been no COVID, if her spirits could have been lifted by being with loved ones, and if she would have made it to her actual hundredth birthday celebration?

When things started to improve at the beginning of 2021, and we had the ability to travel a bit more freely, I had the opportunity to go to Florida during spring break. I can't begin to tell you the joy of getting on a plane again. I remember being at the airport and seeing families and little kids who had to wear masks but who were excited to be going to Disney World. Wearing a mask on the plane is a small price to pay if it enables you to travel.

I was very fortunate that because I am a frontline professor, teaching in person, and because of my age, I was able to get the vaccine early in January 2021. I have to say that since getting vaccinated I have never really worried about getting COVID. I know every person is different, but I feel confident about the vaccine. I'm part of a generation that got the polio vaccine and the flu vaccine, among others. This vaccine is just part of our changing world, and it's giving me the freedom to do the things I love to do.

A lot of gutsy women feel just like me. We've been vaccinated, we take precautions, but we don't want COVID to rule our lives. We're hopeful. The number of people coming to our website is at pre-COVID levels, and the interest in 2022 trips is formidable.

Being a gutsy woman is about deciding how you want to live your life. You can either live it in fear, or you can live it fully without throwing caution to the wind. When travel opened in 2021 our first trip to Iceland sold out in days. Why was that?

I think the number one reason was that I was going on the trip. I think women probably felt if the president and cofounder of the company is comfortable going, they can be too. Number two was that in June 2021, Iceland was at level one (the lowest risk level) and there had not been a COVID death since December 2020. But number three is maybe the most important reason—women were ready to travel again, to have a good time, and to just get away somewhere.

The bottom line is we did live through a global pandemic. It was real. Millions of people worldwide died. And at the same time, millions of people's everyday lives were affected—their work environment, their family environment, their social environment— everything had changed. But it takes a gutsy woman attitude to rise above it and just say, it is what it is.

Remember: It's Your Life...Live IT!

# 9

## *Traveling Again: Pandemic Pioneers*

What does a pandemic travel world look like? It's evolving and while there are still hurdles, I think it will get easier, but you must be prepared. The truth is you have to be prepared for any trip, pandemic or no pandemic. Our first Gutsy Women Travel tour to Iceland, after travel restrictions outside the U.S. were lifted, at the end of June 2021 was a perfect example.

After eighteen long months without travel, we finally had our first trip outside of the U.S. and there was no way I wasn't going to be on it. I felt this was the most important trip we had ever taken. I couldn't wait, and along with my usual trip preparations, I also did something spontaneous. A week before the trip, I decided to change my hair color!

Now for all the women reading this, you know that right before any important event, you do not change your hair color. But after months of not being able to get my hair colored with my usual highlights, I felt I just needed to do something bold, and decided to go with red. I immediately regretted it. Let's just put it down to a little pandemic craziness.

I felt like I had a wig on with my carrottop look. When my sister Camille, who was sharing room accommodations with me on the Iceland trip, arrived at my house to travel to JFK together, I gave her that *don't even ask* look. And even though all the women on the trip said they loved my new red color, it really bothered me the whole week. That was so foolish because I had a lot more important things to worry about on that trip than the color of my hair. But for those who know me well, my hair has always been an issue for me. Idiotic but true.

The nine of us traveling through JFK to Reykjavík were to meet up at the Delta lounge after check-in, but there were no signs of two of our travelers, Chris and her daughter Fei Fei. I kept calling them from the lounge and finally heard from them as we were boarding the flight. They ended up missing the flight because they thought it was the next day!

Our former operator Overseas Adventure Travel (O.A.T.) identified the day we depart the U.S.A. as our start date, but our current operator for Iceland listed the start of the trip as the day we actually landed at our destination, in this case Reykjavík, which was the next day. It was understandably confusing to Chris. In 2022 when we return to O.A.T. as our official tour operator, we will be going back to using our departure date as the start of the trip. Fortunately, our mother and daughter duo traveled the next evening nonstop to Reykjavík from JFK and arrived at the hotel just in time to go to the Retreat Spa Blue Lagoon with the gutsy women and our tour manager.

We were considered pandemic pioneers, one of the first organized tour groups especially for women, to resume travel. One of the reasons we chose Iceland was because it was a level one country, at that time, which meant the COVID rate was very low and there were few restrictions. However, at the time we landed in Reykjavík, even though we were vaccinated, we needed to get tested at the airport upon arrival. We also needed a COVID test before our return to the U.S. airport, but testing at Reykjavík has since been halted, probably because of what happened that fateful day.

When we arrived at Reykjavík, the airport was a zoo. Along with arriving flights with tour passengers and crews, there were several flights with two thousand passengers who were heading out on cruises that landed at the same time as our flight. We were all herded into the same lines for baggage retrieval and then on to the COVID nasal swab testing and vaccination passport verification, which turned out to be a three-hour process. As a point of interest, another group handled by our local Iceland operator had their tour director and a traveler test positive, and the entire group was taken to a quarantine hotel for five days. Thank goodness everyone in our group tested negative, but we didn't leave the airport without drama.

Because of the great number of people arriving, the Reykjavík airport shut down the moving walkways and escalators for safety reasons. We had to use the stairwells that had at least thirty steps to climb while lugging our carry-ons to get to baggage claim. And now the drama begins.

While I was on the flight, the back of my right knee started to hurt. I've had a Baker's cyst there for a few years now, so I didn't give it much thought. But as I was departing the plane and navigating through the airport lines, I found it difficult to walk. When we reached the stairs, my concerned sister suggested we look for an elevator, but I didn't want to separate from our group. She grabbed my carry-on and as I was going up the steps, we heard a pop in the back of my knee. That was the moment my Baker's cyst decided to burst. I could not believe this was happening in real time!

It took an hour to get our luggage. I quickly reached into my bag for more comfortable walking shoes and changed out of my boots. I was able to use the baggage cart for support to help me walk and we proceeded to the COVID testing area that had at least another two-hour line.

Suddenly, we heard an airport page announcement loud and clear, *Will April Merenda please report to the Reykjavík Airport Police Desk!* The rest of the gutsy group arriving with me from JFK looked puzzled as I slowly approached the designated area. That's when I learned that one of the women in our tour group, who had landed from New Orleans, had fainted while waiting in the long, hot line for baggage claim and testing. She had bruised her forehead when she fell. When I got to my client, whom I had never met before, we were all concerned that she seemed disoriented and the medical team wanted me to authorize taking her to the hospital in an ambulance for further tests, which with her permission, I did.

I did not hold back with the police and told them I was not the least bit surprised this happened as the conditions in the arrival area were beyond unacceptable. I also told them about my injury upon arrival and thank goodness, I was able to have all seven of the JFK arrivals in my group follow me directly to the testing area, which saved us about an hour standing on line. It still took our group another hour to get tested and provide our cell phone information so they could text us

*April M. Merenda*

the COVID results. Many of us who paid twenty dollars to use the site our tour operator recommended to secure a verification code to enter the country found that our information was not correct and it had to be updated in the terminal. Welcome to Reykjavík!

After the airport testing drama (and there was more drama to come), we managed to find the other five gutsy women who arrived from various airports and our transfer agent to take us to our hotel, which was about an hour away. The transfer agent noted he couldn't account for three women in our group, and I explained one was on the way to the hospital, but we had her luggage, and two others missed the flight and would need transfers for the same time on the next day.

We arrived at our very nice hotel, the Hotel Klettur, to check in only to find out there were no bellmen due to COVID! I tipped our airport transfer driver extra to assist us. At this point, I could not put any pressure on my right leg and the rest of the group was exhausted from the airport arrival testing process.

We were their first group arrival to this hotel from the U.S. in a while, and the hotel staff was ready and excited to meet us. While checking in, they explained to us that because of COVID, in addition to no bellmen, there was no daily room cleaning, unless you were staying for four nights (we were staying three). That meant if we needed towels, we had to pick them up from the front desk. If we had garbage, we were to leave it in the hallway and then call the front desk to have somebody come pick it up.

How many times have you gone to a hotel and just taken it for granted that there would be a bellman, daily housekeeping, and someone taking your garbage? I have to say, seeing pizza boxes, dirty towels, and garbage bins in the hallways was a bit of a turnoff.

But this was part of the whole new pandemic world. The front desk also explained we were in a designated hotel that allowed guests to walk around the area, but we could not go into a restaurant or storefront until we received our negative COVID test results, which would be texted to us within four to twenty-four hours of our arrival. They shared that as a hotel, they could be fined up to equivalent of $1500 USD if not enforced.

This new reality also set in when I realized there were no amenities in our rooms, no little magazines, and everything was paperless. If you wanted toiletries, like soaps and things like that, you could request it from the front desk, but it was not something that they readily put in the room. In our pandemic travel world, everything is being done to minimize contact and the possible spread of COVID.

My sister got a bucket of ice from the front desk, and I elevated and iced my knee while we both rested for a few hours. After everyone was settled in their rooms, it was time to update the group at our briefing in the lower lobby before our welcome dinner and also have a chance to meet our dedicated tour manager from Iceland.

This was a special trip, so I decided to give out purple welcome gift bags filled with useful items for our Iceland adventure. I brought everything along with me on the plane to prepare the gift bags in my room. I had some great items that included the now famous purple masks and lanyard featured on the book's front cover, snacks courtesy of the Delta Lounge, chocolates, throat lozenges, tissues, I'm Gutsy buttons, a water bottle, and other useful items.

But by now, I could hardly walk, let alone prepare all the gift bags. So I said to Camille, who was willing to help me, that rather than make up the bags in the room, we'd just leave the carry-on at the front desk, bring it to the briefing, and each of the women could help make their own bag.

When I explained the situation at the welcome briefing, the women were just wonderful. They started an assembly line and filled their own bags, and everyone had a great time doing it. I also gave them a Gutsy tote bag for our trip the next day to the Retreat Spa Blue Lagoon for carrying wet bathing suits and toiletries. Everyone was happy and it was another example of how resilient women are.

And by now everyone was concerned about my injury and were offering me anti-inflammatory and pain supplements. Luckily, I travel with ibuprofen and that along with icing was helping immensely. We met our local tour manager at the briefing. She brought maps for the welcome gift bag and reviewed our agenda. Everyone was excited.

We got the good news that our traveler who fainted was being discharged from the hospital. It turns out she was dehydrated from all the bedlam at the airport but had no signs of a concussion from the fall. Fortunately she was able to make it to our welcoming dinner that evening. We arranged a cab to bring her to the hotel, and we waited for her so we could all go together to the welcome dinner. It was walking distance from the hotel, but at this point I couldn't walk much. Thankfully, our tour director had her van at the hotel and arranged to drive all of us to the Gutsy Women welcome dinner at Potturinn & Pannan.

It was one of the best dinners we have ever had, which included the choice of arctic char or lamb that Iceland is so well-known for. I treated everybody to a welcome drink. The staff could not have been nicer. We had the entire restaurant to ourselves, so everyone felt comfortable, and no one had to wear a mask. We were elated to be there, and with all of us chatting away, you would have thought it was sixty people, not a small group of sixteen women.

Each of the women went around the table and introduced herself and shared a little bit about herself and why she took the trip. By the end of the evening, we were all on a first-name basis and ready for our Iceland Explorer adventure. One of our tour members, Danielle, was celebrating her birthday and it was also her first trip on her own without her two young daughters and husband. We planned a special dessert with Icelandic ice cream, and it topped off a great first night. It was a wonderful beginning to a great trip. We were ready. We were the gutsy pandemic pioneers!

When dinner was over, our tour manager dropped off our group at the hotel and then drove me to a twenty-four-hour urgent care facility that fitted me with a knee brace that got me through the rest of the trip. (Thank goodness for the brace because when I returned home and got an MRI, they discovered I had also torn my meniscus and I ended up getting orthoscopic surgery at the end of August.)

The next day was one of those days that will be etched in our memories forever. Thankfully our mother and daughter travelers, Chris and Fei Fei, who had missed the flight the day before, landed. They dodged the bullet that inflicted our arrival. There were no lines, no cruise passengers, and with heavy headwinds, their flight arrived ninety minutes early. They got their negative COVID clearance just in time to join us for the Retreat Spa Blue Lagoon experience.

Our tour manager arrived at our hotel to pick up our group to transfer us to the Retreat Spa and I noticed it was the same van she drove us to dinner in. I asked her where our bus and driver were. She replied she was both the driver and the tour manager, and that this was the vehicle assigned for our group for the entire trip. It was a fifteen-seater passenger vehicle with a seat in the front for the driver and an additional seat next to the driver.

In all my years offering tours, we have never used such a vehicle for a gutsy women group, especially since women have luggage and there was no place within the van to accommodate luggage. (They had to affix a trailer for our bags). We also never had a tour manager as our driver. More importantly, with COVID restrictions and a desire for social distancing, a fifteen-seater van was not ideal for a group of fifteen women. I voiced my reservations about this, which I discuss in Chapter 10, but it was what it was, and we made the best of it.

Just as the world opened up to travel again, we were so fortunate to have a day at the Retreat Spa in Reykjavík at the Blue Lagoon. It's considered one of the best spas in the world where we would enjoy spa treatments and relax in the waters of the Blue Lagoon, which is fed by geothermal seawater from deep under the lava. The waters are rich in silica, algae, and minerals that soften and rejuvenate the skin.

When we arrived at the Retreat Spa, it was like landing on *Fantasy Island*. The staff was waiting for us, and we were escorted to the private dressing area and given our own dressing rooms that accommodated two women. Inside our rooms, we discovered all the Blue Lagoon products that were ours to take home. They included mud facials, cleansing creams, body lotion, and shampoos. We had our own showers and were able to change into our bathing suits in privacy as opposed to the public areas of the Blue Lagoon. It was equipped with blow-dryers, flat irons, and other hair tools.

I had an extra surprise for our group when I shared that Gutsy Women was treating each of them to a thirty-minute hydro massage in the thermal waters of the Blue Lagoon and had made reservations months ago with a fabulous Retreat Spa attendant named Thuri. Thank heavens she and I methodically planned this day out with the massage appointments well in advance as the spa was totally sold out and no appointments would have been available had we waited until our arrival.

I wanted to treat our tour manager to a day at the spa as she had never been to the Retreat Spa but there was no availability. She explained her office needed her due to the other group now in quarantine. She wished us a great day and said she would return to pick us up when our spa day was over.

With everything we had gone through due to COVID leading up to this trip and with all the drama upon our arrival, we deserved some extra pampering. The spa experience was just fabulous. There's a ritual that starts with a body scrub and a mud bath. Then you have oils and body creams applied. After that there are plunging pools of your choice, which range from lukewarm to freezing. And then there was our half-hour massage in the thermal healing waters. You could stay in the waters as long as you like and take in the sights.

We were also treated to a complimentary alcoholic or wellness drink, which usually cost between twenty-five and thirty dollars. It was just wonderful to order our beverages using our special bracelets while in the thermal waters. Guests are prohibited from taking photos on the premises, but the staff is allowed to take photos and you'll see some of our joyous moments in the photo gallery.

I'll never forget our dinner that night at the spa. I had reserved a table for our group at their Lava restaurant overlooking the lagoon. I was the last one to arrive at the table, as I was thanking Thuri and the spa attendants for executing all of our appointments flawlessly. I looked around at everyone, and I couldn't believe what a difference that five hours in a spa had made.

Everyone was relaxed and glowing from their treatments and in the best mood. The manager of the restaurant came over and commented that we were one of the best groups they'd ever had. I laughingly said, "I'm sure you say that to all the groups." He replied quite sincerely that we really were and treated us each to a glass of champagne.

Overjoyed and filled with emotions, I got up to make a little speech. "For the past eighteen months our lives have been so restricted. I want you to look back on this day and be able to say with bragging rights that when we were able to travel again, you were one of the first gutsy travelers, you were one of our gutsy pandemic pioneers, and you were able to experience the amazing Retreat Spa in the Blue Lagoon." Other women got up and spoke about what an unforgettable day it was. It was yet another special beginning to a great trip.

The next morning, some of the women got up early to do a special trip with our tour manager to visit the smoldering volcanic site. They drove about thirty minutes to a designated parking area and then hiked up to the volcano and then walked back down. As much as I wanted to go, I knew that with my injury I would never be able to walk on the gravel and sustain the hike. But the women who went were thrilled and we have pictures in the photo gallery. As a group, we departed our hotel around noon and drove to the Children's Water-fall and learned about the legend behind the name of this enchanting spot.

We then headed to the warmest thermal spring to soak and relax in the Krauma Thermal Baths, and while it wasn't the Blue Lagoon, we really enjoyed it. We had to bring our towels from the hotel so our Gutsy tote bags came in handy again.

As we were leaving the spa, we spotted a beautiful field filled with gorgeous purple flowers with the majestic mountains in the back-ground. Our tour director said it was the perfect setting for a group photo. We had asked the women to bring their purple masks from the welcome gift bag and that's where we took the now famous picture that's on the cover of this book. We all had the mask on for the first photo, and for the next one, we joyously took them off in a throwing them to the wind gesture. It went viral on social media with literally tens of thousands of views. It evoked the spirit of being able to travel again. That's when we realized how important it was to become the Gutsy Women pandemic pioneers.

There was another treat that day. Believe it or not, in addition to arctic char, Iceland is known for its hot dogs. We stopped at the St-aldrid Food Stand, which serves hot dogs and fish-and-chips. It was a wonderful local experience.

We spent the following day touring the city of Reykjavík. The next day, after we all met as a group and made our appointments for our COVID test prior to our return to the U.S.A., we would be on the road traveling to remote inner parts of Iceland, which weren't near an air-port or a hospital. The morning we were leaving, our tour director asked me how our traveler who fainted and fell at the airport was feeling. She assured me she was okay and was ready to continue on our journey to the middle of the farmlands of Iceland.

We arrived at a quaint little eco-farmhouse, in the town of Hver-agerdi, for our first overnight stay. It was surreal. You could see how the pandemic had really affected a lot of these places. With very little business in months, they were operating with a lean staff. The owner checked us in and her son was the bellman. That night, we had our welcome dinner there.

The following day we were going to go to the Westman Islands (Vestmannaeyjar), to the island called Heimaey. It's surrounded by

*April M. Merenda*

fifteen other uninhabited islands. There are two volcanoes and eruptions are a big part of Westman Islands history. It has unique foliage and a bird sanctuary. This is where Iceland's famous puffins are from, and everybody was excited to see them. The day excursion included taking the ferry back and forth, visiting the museum and shops, and dining in the local restaurants.

That morning, our traveler who had fallen at the airport told her roommate that she was feeling a little warm. Now the farmhouse did not have air-conditioning, which is commonplace in Iceland. When I went to check on her, she seemed fine to me, and I thought it was just that her room was a little warm. But keep in mind, we were in pandemic fear mode. Our tour manager asked the proprietor of the farm for a thermometer, and it showed she had a 102-degree temperature. I didn't trust the thermometer, which the proprietor admitted was old, so we made the decision that before we started panicking, we'd call an ambulance.

Their emergency team came quickly. I told them she had COVID in the past, was vaccinated, and we all tested negative for COVID when we arrived. I also told them about her dehydration and fainting at the airport. They took her temperature, which was 99 degrees and agreed with me that it wasn't COVID, but since her temperature was slightly elevated, they said she should go to the hospital to be checked out.

That's when the tour director said she needed to leave to get the rest of the group to the ferry. Remember my reservations about having a tour manager and the bus driver being the same person? This is a major reason why it's not a great idea when you are traveling with a group. So as much as I wanted to visit the Westman Islands, I agreed to stay behind and go the hospital in the ambulance with my client so our tour manager could take the rest of our group to the ferry and then on to the Westman Islands tour.

I tried to make our client feel comfortable during our hour ride to the hospital, joking that she should write a paper on how she toured the various hospitals within Iceland! Let me add a note here about how wonderful the emergency team was. And tall. Iceland has one of the tallest populations in the world, and everyone we met, including our tour manager, was six feet tall or close to it. And since I've shrunk over the years to only five feet one inch, they seem even taller. When the emergency team stepped out of the ambulance, they looked like

Barbie and Ken out of central casting for a movie. Icelanders are very glamourous, even in emergency gear.

I have been to emergency rooms and hospitals in various countries, but I have never seen one run as well as this one. They took her in immediately and were very attentive. I filled out her forms, which was very easy to do. She had every test possible and within an hour and a half the doctor had her results. With her permission, I was allowed to hear his diagnosis. He said it looked like she might have picked up some kind of viral infection, maybe even at the airport when she was in line with so many people. Normally he wouldn't do anything, but since she was in a group setting—and to alleviate everyone's fears—he prescribed a three-day Z-Pak. He said she could continue to travel with the group but to distance herself for the first twenty-four hours. After that, she'd be fine as would those around her.

That night when the group returned from the ferry, our tour manager had a surprise for me. Our van had a broken landing and I found it very hard, along with other petite women, to climb in and out of the van. While in town, she had bought a step stool to facilitate getting in and out of the vehicle. It helped. The vehicle was not to our satisfaction, but we made the best of it.

We had dinner at the farmhouse again and had dinner delivered to the room of our tour member with the viral infection. The next day, she wore her mask in the van and sat in the front seat next to our driver who also wore her mask. We left the farmhouse after two nights and thankfully all of us were able to continue on our journey to see the glaciers and the waterfalls.

On the way to our lodgings, picturesquely located by the edge of the Vatnajökull glacier in Skaftafell National Park, we visited the stunning Skógafoss waterfall, where some of our group climbed the nearby staircase for some breathtaking views. That afternoon we cruised between jagged icebergs in Jökulsárlón Glacier Lagoon.

I've been to the beautiful glaciers in Alaska, but the glaciers in Iceland are unbelievable. We had the opportunity to taste glacier water, and it is the purest water you will ever experience. While Iceland is expensive because everything has to be imported, the one thing that is not imported is bottled water. One of the items in my gift bags was a water bottle and everywhere you go in Iceland they have water stations where you can fill up. That curtails plastic bottles, and Iceland is very much into sustainability.

We went back to our lodge in the glaciers for our last night before returning to Reykjavík. Normally on the last night of our trips, the group wants to go someplace fun with local music and dancing. But that wasn't going to happen in the middle of nowhere and during a pandemic.

However, I always travel with my Bluetooth speaker. I asked twenty-one-year-old Fei Fei to help me set up a playlist. She asked everyone what their favorite dancing songs were and she loaded them up on my phone. I went to the hotel and asked them if they had a private room they could give us, which they agreed to do. Then I told everyone to grab their favorite beverage, bring some snacks, and join us for a private party.

We put on the playlist with everyone's favorite songs, and before you knew it, we were all up dancing. We danced, and we danced, and we danced. Even our tour director joined in. She said in all of her years managing trips, she had never experienced anything like it. She also brought a bottle of Reyka vodka, which is considered the best vodka in the world. Everybody got a little shot along with a piece of fermented shark on a toothpick that goes along with the shot. It smelled and tasted horrible. We have a funny picture in the photo gallery of a few of us making horrible faces after tasting it. But it was part of the tradition. It was such a spontaneous and fun evening and, to this day, the women say it was one of the best nights of their life.

At one point during the evening, I went around the room and asked every woman what part of the trip impressed or empowered her most. What was remarkable is that no two answers were the same. That's when I realized the trip had exceeded everyone's expectations. We all had a different takeaway, but we were so grateful to have had the experience and to travel again.

We always like to have a hidden treasure or a surprise on every trip. It had been a long journey and now we were leaving the glacier area and heading back to Reykjavík. It's a good five-hour journey, and of course, you do have to stop. The surprise was our stop at a private farm owned by a woman with the most beautiful Icelandic horses. We couldn't ride them, but the women had a chance to go to the stables, pet the gorgeous horses, and take pictures.

Then we went back to the house for an incredible buffet lunch. Everybody said it was the best meal of the trip. There was arctic char, of course, which we never got tired of because there are so many ways to prepare it. She had made all kinds of delicious desserts and many other different items. She also served the best coffee (Gevalia). We loved being in her home with her gracious hospitality.

But the surprises weren't over. A little bit down the road there was a sheep farm and wool tannery, where a community of women make textiles from old-fashioned spinning wheels. They make beautiful sweaters, rugs, and other handmade items. We had a chance to see how everything is made, and to hear the women had learned the art of spinning from their grandmothers and their great grandmothers. Many of the women in our group bought handmade towels and other little things from this very special place.

We made one more stop at another popular hot dog stand, Pylsu-vagninn Laugardal, near Reykjavík University. We got to try their famous Pylsa hot dog. Now I'm from New York, and we have Nathan's and Coney Island, but I have to say it was the best hot dog I've ever had. Then we returned to the same hotel we stayed in on arrival. We knew the drill with the towels, etc. Usually, we have our farewell dinner on the last night, but our dance party was our farewell. So, everyone was on their own to dine wherever they liked.

There were five of us from New York who ended up eating at Hlemmur Mathöll, Reykjavík's first food hall, inspired by the great European food markets. It's located inside a unique building that used to house Reykjavík's main bus terminal. They have five different restaurant vendors offering the best food Iceland has to offer. There's also a bar you can order drinks from. It turned out to be great and relatively inexpensive. So, despite Iceland's reputation for being very expensive, you can find places with reasonable prices.

A few observations about Reykjavík. It's a vibrant city, with a lot of young people. There are trendy restaurants and bars, as well as shops and museums. It also has a downside, and that is signs of drug use. We did see several strung out people on the streets (it was the only place where we saw this) but there's also a lot of police presence that seems to keep things in control and safe.

Iceland is now becoming one of the top tourist destinations worldwide. But Iceland and other countries alike need to be resilient as this is a must for travel in a COVID world. You have to be prepared and flexible.

All things considered, and despite the drama throughout the trip, this group of gutsy pandemic pioneers did great! Our tour manager was one of the best we had the pleasure to work with over the twenty years of our tours. We had a wonderful adventure and made memories for a lifetime. On a happy note, since I missed the Westman Islands tour, I plan to return to Iceland with a Gutsy Women group to see the northern lights and the Westman Islands in 2023.

# 10

## *Best Practices*

Throughout this book I've shared my journey as an entrepreneur, as a travel expert, and as a professor. I've also shared lessons I've learned along the way. In this chapter, I'd like to highlight suggestions for best practices and advice for the travel industry, entrepreneurs, and students.

### Advice for Country Authorities and Tour Operators

COVID is still here and it may be for years to come. But we're learning to live with it. I think the vaccines are doing a good job protecting us from dying, as are social distancing and mask wearing. Our leaders need to present our new reality in a more positive way so that people understand that they can protect themselves and others and resume their lives. We will have to learn from the good and the bad, but we need to keep moving forward.

We're all figuring out this new dynamic, but from my experience traveling to Iceland I believe the following recommendations will make travelers feel more at ease and more likely to travel again.

**Create separate COVID testing lines.** To avoid the long wait we had at the airport in Iceland for our COVID tests because thousands of cruise passengers arrived at the same time, local authorities should create separate lines and testing areas for cruise passengers, rail passengers, and airline passengers.

**List where to get free COVID tests**. A negative COVID test is also required to return to the U.S. from many countries. Travelers should be provided with a listing of free government test sites as well as those that charge a fee. There are sites that are making money off testing people who could have received the test for free.

**An accurate infrared thermometer.** Our thermometer incident in the farmhouse in the middle of Iceland made it clear that every tour operator, every major hotel, and every B and B needs to have an accurate infrared thermometer that you just point to the forehead or your wrist for an accurate reading.

**Provide social distancing during tours.** This is one way to keep us safer. Therefore, tour operations should use larger passenger buses to accommodate fewer people. Fifteen people should not be in a fifteen-person van. They should be traveling on a thirty-person bus.

**Emergency contingency plan and task force.** During the height of the crisis, there was so much conflicting information no one was confident about what we were hearing. We learned a lot of things during this crisis that I'm hoping we can work on in the future. At the top of my list, I believe we need some type of central point where our industry can get reliable and updated information. I've floated the idea of creating a nonpolitical task force whose priority is keeping people safe, whether it's COVID or any type of health crisis.

**Make travelers feel safe.** Our experience in Iceland was a great example. They had a plan in place that included free testing at the airport, texting you with results, and easy procedures for testing for your return. It worked like clockwork. In public places people were cautious and social distanced. We had a great time and did everything on our agenda. We were not fearful in any sense. There are opportunities for destinations who create smart practices like Iceland to become popular with travelers again by doing things right and making visitors feel welcomed and safe.

*****

## Advice for Travelers

**Arrive to the airport early**. When the airline says arrive three hours in advance, take it seriously. On our return to the airport for the trip home from Iceland, we had to stand on line to show the agents our negative COVID test results. There was no electronic check-in, and even though our airline was very organized, this was still very time-consuming.

**Travel insurance.** It's very low cost and will cover many emergencies medical expenses and repatriation if you get ill while traveling. For example, it will cover COVID tests at a medical facility. Our client in Iceland who had to be taken to the hospital had travel insurance and it covered her more than $2,000 in medical bills and the $190 cab ride back to the farmhouse. Repatriation insurance provides emergency medical treatment and transportation home if you are injured or ill in another country.

**Know your tour date versus your airline departure date**. We are time deprived and drawn in various directions and sometimes do not pay attention to details that affect us most. See Chapter 5, It's About the Journey, when one client missed their flight.

**Know where you are staying**. Have the information on your person. See Chapter 6, Where's Melissa?

**Don't leave belongings behind.** Heed our advice and always double check your closet and drawers before checking out.

**Have a color copy of your passport.** ID is always required when using your credit card or verifying your vaccination passport. I also witnessed a situation when my client forgot her passport in her river cruise safe and was allowed to depart with a color copy of her passport and the cruise line overnighted the original to her next destination

**Personal health.** Pack a first aid kit. Bring any personal medications, prescriptions, prescription glasses, hearing aids and chargers, contact lenses, and solution. Bring sunscreen, lip balm, and insect repellent. Other items to include are antihistamines, insect bite cream, travel sickness pills, rehydration powder, and anti-diarrhea pills.

**Money.** Always have more than one credit card. Have a money belt or pouch for safekeeping. During the tsunami in Southeast Asia, there were no working ATMs so always carry some cash with you for emergencies.

**Sleeping.** Have an eye mask, ear plugs, and an alarm clock (if your cell phone doesn't have one.)

**Personal Items**. Travel pillow. A day pack. Pen and paper. Electrical adaptor for the country you are traveling to. Small sewing kit. Check that your mobile phone has international roaming access and download WhatsApp. Bring an empty bottle of water to fill up at water stations.

**Clothing**. Check the weather for the country you are going to. Always be prepared for rain. Always have a shawl or wrap for the plane. Layer your outfits to adjust to changing temperatures throughout the day, and always mix and match outfits. My favorite saying is "No one remembers the bottom." So, you can interchange tops with a pair of slacks or skirt to expand your outfit selections on tour.

*****

## Advice for Entrepreneurs and Students

### Celebrate milestones.

I've always believed in celebrating milestones. Just as we celebrate milestone birthdays and anniversaries in our personal lives, celebrating your company's milestones or career milestones is just as important. We've always celebrated our Gutsy Women Travel milestones, especially our birthdays. Here are highlights of some of our milestone celebrations.

In November 2011, I hosted a tenth birthday party weekend for Gutsy Women Travel right where it all began, New York City. I remember it as if it was yesterday. It remains one of the happiest times of my life.

The festivities began with a hosted musical performance of renowned singer Giada Valenti. The following day, I contracted Lee Gelber, the most informed tour guide in New York City and hosted a walking tour of Central Park. After the tour we arranged complimentary makeovers at Chanel in Bergdorf Goodman. The evening was topped off with a buffet dinner at the Penthouse of the Skyline Hotel, which has one of the best views of Manhattan at night. Seventy-five gutsy women gathered to celebrate our milestone. They shared their stories too. One in particular stands out.

Gutsy Annette treated herself to the 2009 Amalfi Coast trip and wore the only possession she retained after Hurricane Katrina—a pair of jeweled flat shoes that were on the top of her closet and unscathed from the floodwaters. She wore them that same night she spoke at our tenth anniversary dinner and her story inspired most in the room.

The tenth anniversary celebration reinforced our mission statement that we are far more a travel company. We are a movement—a movement that gives women permission to put themselves at the top of their list.

We celebrated our thirteenth birthday with a Gutsy Women trip to Costa Rica. Our Sweet Sixteen was celebrated again in New York City. We had seventy-five women attending, and we left in anticipation of what we will host when Gutsy turns twenty-one in November 2022!

## Reward customer loyalty.

Here's what we do. After the first trip, Gutsy Women travelers receive a 5 percent savings. If they share their testimony on their travels and it nets us a new client, they receive a bonus gift of a one-hundred-dollar discount on their next trip. Finally, if women book and share with a friend or come solo and agree to be matched if single rooms are sold out, we extend another hundred-dollar savings. It's important to thank those who are responsible for your growth with a rewards program. It's worked well for us.

## Transparency.

Always be honest and aboveboard with your client base. Explain your policies so they understand them. If you cross that line, your customers will never entrust you with their business again.

*April M. Merenda*

**Be true to who you are.**

Develop your own sense of style and be comfortable in your skin. At the same time, it's important to exude a sense of who you are.

**Have a plan.**

I have met few business owners who planned to fail, but I have met many who failed because they had no plan. You must have a plan as a start-up or even for your career development goals. It's important to understand how to put together a strategic plan so you know where you're going. A marketing plan will help you get there, but you need to know who you are marketing to and most important what you are marketing and how it meets your market's needs. If you are starting a business, you need cash flow resources to tide you over until you turn a profit.

# 11

## *Be Kind to Yourself*

Of all my lessons learned, being kind to yourself is perhaps the most important.

Throughout the years, I've seen the restorative power of travel for women. We wear many hats, we have demanding lives, and we often put everyone else's needs ahead of our own, especially those who are caregivers. I've introduced you to several of our gutsy women travelers who are caregivers and allow themselves a much-needed self-care break by taking a trip. Since the year 2000, I was a caregiver to my own mother, so I can always relate to these women. And we're not alone.

It's estimated that 66 percent of caregivers are midlife women who work outside of the home and devote at least twenty hours a week providing care, usually to their mothers. While I truly considered it an honor to care for the woman who brought me into this world and raised me, it wasn't always easy and it was challenging, especially during the pandemic.

I have three sisters and a brother, and they would help when they could. My sister Denise lives in South Carolina and would try to travel to New York when I was called out of town. She would work out a schedule with our other siblings. My sister Camille, who lives on Long Island, works full-time, and is a mother of three would try to visit at least once a week. My brother, Ed, who lives upstate tried to visit every month and make our mother lunch and bring homemade soup. He would often bring her brother Bob, which she enjoyed. My eldest sister Diana is a cancer survivor, and has her own underlining conditions, so personal visits, especially during COVID were difficult. Everyone did what they could. But I was the sibling responsible for our mother and sometimes I would feel overwhelmed and sometimes I would lose my patience.

Since her ninety-ninth birthday in February 2020, Gilda had been confined to home hospice care due to her acute dementia and dysphagia, an end-of-life eating disorder. During the pandemic, I taught remotely from our home in Valley Stream through the spring semester. I got to spend time with her, go for walks while she was confined to a wheelchair, and at the same time attend to gifting all the material and sewing artifacts she had collected over the years to various organizations. In a strange sense, the pandemic allowed me the resilience to prepare for what was to come.

I was given the opportunity to teach in person at our Staten Island campus for the fall 2020 semester. It was a difficult decision, as I knew she could pass any day, but I decided to go back to the classroom. I felt it was important for the students and after everything this generation went through during the pandemic, they deserved in-person teaching. In my heart, I hoped that if she had all her faculties, she would have embraced me going back to the classroom and would not have wanted me to stay at home.

Appreciating the importance of milestone celebrations, I hosted a faux one hundredth birthday party in her home on August 21, six months prior to her real milestone birthday and just prior to the fall semester commencing. It was a small gathering with masks required and social distancing enforced. My brother, sisters, a few close neighbors, along with her hospice aides and her pastoral care coordinator for MJHS home hospice, Reverend Father Kyrian C. Echekwu (PhD), shared in the festivities.

I have never seen my mother look as happy as she did that day. I truly believe she thought she had made it to one hundred years, which no one in her family had succeeded in reaching. She even tried to say a few words and managed to express, *I love you all*, which brought tears of joy to everyone present. It was a great day celebrating her life in her presence and I will be forever thankful that we shared that experience with her.

So, I returned to in-person teaching, and just after classes were ending over the Thanksgiving break, my mother passed away.

I was overcome with guilt. I should have, could have been there the whole time. But it was the chairman of my division who reminded me that my mother would not have wanted it any other way. She knew I had been there for her, and that I did the best I could. And she was happy that I was trying to live my best life.

So much of this book is about best practices and lessons learned, and I want to give some counseling to all the caregivers out there.

As I have said, it was an honor for me to be my mother's caregiver but that didn't mean it was easy. From time to time I would feel angry and lose my patience. My first piece of advice is do not beat yourself up. Don't look back at things you wish you had done differently; it will fill you with needless remorse.

By the end of August 2020, my mother had been in hospice care for six months. Every month, the hospice nurse and social worker would come to see her and review how she was doing in her home. By the end of October, the hospice team needed to do an assessment with the hospice doctor. The hospice nurse and social worker came to our home, and the doctor joined us via telemedicine video call. Gilda could barely stand on her own and wasn't eating much. To my surprise, the doctor thought my mother looked great and noted she hadn't lost any further weight since the last review. The doctor felt they might have to take her off hospice! This gave me a false sense of hope and made me lose sight of the end-of-life signs that hospice reviews with caregivers that were soon to come.

So, when two weeks went by after the assessment and my mother wasn't eating, I got angry and asked her why. I was not focused on the end-of-life stages. And then the following week, she was suddenly craving sweets, another sign missed. The night before Thanksgiving, her whole body giggled when I told her she had consumed two melted Creamsicles! I stayed with her until the wee hours of the morning as she talked and talked. It was a wonderful lasting memory seeing her glowing, radiant smile boasting a full mouth of perfect teeth (Gilda never had a cavity and was proud of it). This boost in energy is what the hospice experts describe as the *surge*. The next day was Thanksgiving and she barely spoke. Sadly, my mother passed away the Sunday morning following our Thanksgiving holiday, ironically one month after hospice thought they may need to terminate their services.

And of course, after she passed, my angry words over her not eating were all I could think about. Reverend Father Kyrian told me to stop being so hard on myself. It was a tremendous comfort when he said to me, "You were there for your mother, and right now you need to be there for you and be your own best friend."

That was such important advice and I want to share it with anyone who is a caregiver—be your own best friend and be kind to yourself.

After I got past the guilt, I realized I had all this energy. Where had it come from? Then it dawned on me that for decades I had been devoted to my mother. I did her shopping, I cooked for her, I helped bath her. I had dealt with her doctors for years and while watching her decline with dementia, I would try to talk with her or watch a movie with her and just be there for her. All the energy that had been required for years was now freed up. It was an amazing realization, and I've channeled some of that energy into making this book a reality.

I would counsel other caregivers to do the same once their caregiving days are over. Take that energy and direct it into something positive, or maybe into something you might have neglected doing for yourself.

My final piece of advice is to realize that caregiving is the most honorable thing you can do. As hard as it is with the time, effort, and emotions that are involved, remember it is a reward that you should not take lightly. Be proud of yourself and know that there are other people in the same situation. Find that community of people who understand what you are going through.

I cannot say enough good things about the MJHS home hospice group who was there for my mother through the end but was also there for me. Their Reverend Father Kyrian, Pastoral Care for MJHS, came to our home every Friday during her hospice confinement throughout the pandemic and prayed with us up until the Friday after Thanksgiving when he administered Gilda's last rites. And with no ability to host a Mass for Gilda during her bereavement due to COVID restrictions, Reverend Father Kyrian, joined by Father Cummins from St. John's University, hosted a prayer service during her wake service. After my mother passed, I joined the MJHS bereavement group, and it was very healing. I could never have gone through that difficult time without them.

And my last piece of advice is to treat yourself to a wonderful get-away that restores and soothes your soul, just like I did when travel restrictions lifted, and I went to Florida and Iceland. After all, It's Your Life...Live IT!

*April M. Merenda*

# 12

## *Full Circle*

Not everyone is fortunate enough to find a career they love. I was lucky enough to find two careers I love. Or should I say they found me.

When I graduated from St. John's University in 1975, hospitality courses didn't exist. I never imagined a career in travel, but shortly after graduation, the travel industry found me. Then nearly twenty-five years later, St. John's started a hospitality program, and academia found me.

The St. John's University alumni department, which does a very good job of keeping track of its alumni, reached out to me not long after I was back in New York and working for Icahn Associates. They wanted to meet with me. I invited them to our office for the meeting and also introduced them to Carl and Gail Icahn.

I was excited to learn that the SJU College of Professional Studies (CPS) was starting a hospitality program and was honored to be invited to join their college's advisory board. Through Icahn's travel business, I was also happy to put together an assortment of alumni travel benefits that included discounted airline tickets, discounts at major hotel chains, and special deals at Las Vegas casinos owned by Icahn at that time, which included the Sands and the Stratosphere Hotel.

I enjoyed being on the CPS advisory board. My role was to provide feedback from the hospitality and travel sector on how academia could help fill their needs in the business world.

In 2006, when I became the owner of Gutsy Women, I resigned

from the board because I felt staying on would be a conflict of interest. Then another angel came into my life.

Like Gail Golden-Icahn, Dani Pipano, and Rolf Van Deurzen, Kathleen Vouté MacDonald, Dean of the College of Professional Studies at St. John's University at the time, saw something in me that was about to be another life-changer. I had been teaching courses in hospitality at St. John's as an adjunct professor since August 2004. We had stayed in touch, and when I told her I had outsourced the Gutsy Women Travel operation to Gate 1 Travel, she had a proposition for me. She felt that my business acumen, my experience in the travel industry, my connections, and the fact that I was an alumna would make me the perfect person to facilitate placement for academic internship opportunities for CPS students.

It was a new full-time position, and Dean MacDonald needed assurances that I was not running the day-to-day operations of Gutsy Women. I gave her my assurance and expressed how excited I was about this opportunity and grateful that she was willing to hire me as an industry professional to contribute to the academic world.

She got approval to create the position, and in January 2007, I started my full-time position at St. John's University, my alma mater, as an assistant to the dean/external affairs. And that's when my love affair for mentoring students started.

My job was to meet with CPS students who were majoring in communications, hospitality, health care, criminal justice, and sports management and, based on my numerous industry contacts, set up opportunities for them to secure academic internships. It was a match made in heaven.

I loved interacting with the students and am very proud to say that in the ten years in that the role, I have helped facilitate the internship placement of a thousand students in organizations that included Madison Square Garden, Barclays Center, ABC, BET, CBS, NBC, NY Hospitals, ATF, and numerous hotels, food establishments, and event planning companies.

I complemented the process by hosting an annual internship fair every October with the help of our division secretaries on our SJU Queens campus featuring approximately one hundred companies seeking interns that gave students the opportunity to meet with perspective employers. I often themed the fair with either fall decorations or a Halloween theme. Everyone loved coming to our internship fairs—students, faculty, and employers. The job was a blessing, and I was giving back and making a difference, which is part of the Vincentian mission of our university.

The internship fair in 2010 in particular sticks out in my mind. We were trying to grow the hospitality management program that included food and beverage courses. At that time, the reality cooking shows and competitions were on the rise. One of the finalists on *The Next Iron Chef* was Jehangir Mehta. I decided to make a reservation at his restaurant, Graffiti, in the East Village so I could meet him.

We discussed the importance of providing opportunities for aspiring students and he generously agreed to do a hands-on cooking demonstration at a dedicated section of the upcoming internship fair to be held at St. John's University Taffner Hall. It was a dynamic and memorable event. Hundreds of students and faculty, along with company representatives, enjoyed this once-in-a-lifetime opportunity.

The importance of internship placements soon became a major role for St. John's University Career Services Center. Since the College of Professional Studies had created a major in hospitality management, I left my external affairs position and was hired in January 2017 as an assistant professor/industry professional in the hospitality management program. I am on an industry track to obtain tenure by September 2024.

I have brought my decades of experience in the business world to academia and now into my classroom. My transition to becoming an assistant professor enabled me to also have a faculty mentor. In many ways my mentor has been another angel in my life.

Over the years, I have gained respect among students as a hands-on professor with international experience and a business approach to my classes. The end goal is to secure a job in the hospitality industry or suitable industry to utilize their skills. I schedule industry professionals as guest speakers, we take field trips to various companies, and I help secure academic internships. During the spring break in 2019, sixteen hospitality students took a trip to Italy with me where we met industry experts throughout our visit to Rome and Bologna.

I truly believe that an education at St. John's University not only helps mold students as individuals but prepares them for the real world and helps them secure meaningful employment in their field of study. I am very proud to say most of our graduating students in May 2021 ended up with excellent job placements, even in these tough times.

In 2019, another opportunity came my way. I was asked to participate in developing a graduate program in hospitality at St. John's University, culminating in a master's degree in international hospitality management (MSIHM). At the time of this writing, we have completed our second year of offering this master's, and we've doubled the number of students enrolled—during a pandemic when the hospitality industry has been decimated. How has that happened?

One of the reasons is that I ingrain in my students to never retreat. I share my story of starting a travel business right after 9/11. We had to keep moving forward then, just as we do now with the pandemic. I advise them that this is a good opportunity to build up their skills and their marketability to an employer. A lot of people left the industry during the pandemic, and many are not coming back. Now is an excellent time to look for a key position in hospitality. It's also a truism that with a master's degree, students can earn up to 30 percent more than a student without a graduate degree, and they will be first in line for an interview too.

My innovative approach to the hospitality program has created opportunities to bring students and the hospitality industry together. I've organized many events with New York City Tourism, including a recent event at One World Trade Center. Our students had the chance to meet some amazing people in the industry, and the attendees met students who are ready to hit the ground running.

I also reinvented some of our courses—for example our food and beverage class. The pandemic has resulted in life-altering changes in the way we live, the way we eat, and the way we dine.

In the past you'd run out of the house and grab a bagel or a Danish and a cup of coffee on your way to work or school. Now, with remote work or remote school, people have time for breakfast at home, and that's actually led to healthier eating. The sales of nutritional cereals, alternative dairy products like oat milk, and fresh fruits went through the roof. People are buying herbal teas, energy drinks, and food with vitamins. Sales of organic everything continue to rise. Food delivery changed too with delivery service companies like Instacart, and Door-Dash soaring in popularity.

Another big change within the hospitality industry during the pan-

*April M. Merenda*

demic, which we've incorporated into our classes, is how hotels are now managing their guests. You'll no longer find chocolate on your pillow or magazines in your room. Because of COVID, that's gone. Now you have hand sanitizers and complimentary masks. These changes will stay with us in the future as we learn to live with COVID, not be afraid of it, and embrace our lives.

During the darkest days of COVID, hotel managers could have thrown up their hands in despair but they didn't. Many hotels used their space to feed the indigent and to house hospital workers. They also used that time to look at their bottom lines and make tough decisions about what they needed to do to become profitable. Hotel managers are now looking for students who not only understand the sales and marketing aspects of their company but the revenue management as well.

In our master's program, we now feature revenue management optimization, along with marketing and sales. When our students graduate, these skills will give them an advantage because this is exactly what hotel managers need now.

Our international hospitality management master's program also includes courses in analytics, taught by a professor, Dr. Parks. He takes a subject that can be very intimidating but makes it so enjoyable to learn that the students embrace it.

By contracting industry professionals like me, St. John's has been able to provide a new dimension to our programs that combines the pursuit of higher learning with career marketability. Not only are we making learning enjoyable, but applicable to what students need when they graduate.

I love working with young people and sharing my real-world experience as a hospitality and travel expert, and as an entrepreneur. They appreciate hearing my stories and I appreciate hearing theirs. My classroom is always a lively exchange of ideas and the students have enriched my life.

One of my favorite classes is International Destinations and Culture, and it is a favorite of students as well. It tackles the need to be empathetic to other people's cultures. We are a true melting pot, and we don't have to look any further than our own student body to see the diversity.

The class touches on diversity in a very seamless way by gathering stories of immigrants who've come to the United States of America. I often provide examples like sharing the experience of immigrants eating their first McDonald's hamburger. Fast food and the way we eat on the run here is a big culture shock. The course delves into cultural diversity and how social media has also affected cultural traditions.

One of the assignments for this class and my graduate classes in International Hospitality Management is for each of them to share their own cultural footprint as a digital story. I ask them to tell me their story and complement it with a picture. It could be a picture with their pet, in their favorite outfit, with their family, with their friends, or doing something they enjoy that represents them, and then write their story and share it with the class. While teaching remotely, this exercise has also served as a great catalyst to foster camaraderie. Here are a few of my favorites from students who gave me permission to their digital stories.

### Digital Story #1

Success is not a materialistic matter but the fulfillment of life in how we have a positive impact on others and live our days to the fullest.

As a senior majoring in hospitality management with a minor in business administration in St. John's undergraduate program, I'm honored and proud to be on the path of pursuing the degree of International Hospitality Management Master of Science (M.S.)

Coming to the United States from another country when I was merely a high school kid, I was at the stage of being lost with multiple challenges including the new environment, language barrier, and cultural differences. The door to St. John's has led me to become more independent and confident in myself. Since my freshman year, I have started my journey of looking for my dream and passion. I would like my life to carry a meaning in which I create positive impacts on others' lives, and the hospitality industry turns out to be a great fit. The word *hospitality* speaks for itself, which carries the mission of providing care, love, and respect through our services to others.

I believe that maturity is to kill yourself of yesterday by improving yourself daily. By joining the International Hospitality Management program, I aspire to learn more experience from professors and doing more research about related fields. Opportunities only come for people who are ready, thus, I would like to prepare myself for the future and challenges ahead in the best possible way through this program.

## Digital Story #2

My name is Pedro, and I was born in Brooklyn, New York. I come from a Dominican family who immigrated from the Dominican Republic in the 80s. My family comes from a farming background and once they immigrated to the U.S., they worked in low-skilled labor employment such as in manufacturing factories. My mother's first job once she arrived in the U.S. was manufacturing image writer cassettes that printers used to use. As a teenager she arrived seeking a better life than that she had in the countryside. Having to raise a family, she had no time to further her education. She always had to work to survive and continued providing for her kids. My mother used to always tell me as a child if she would have decided to study and go to school, she probably will not be struggling so much today. These words have always motivated me to become a better person.

When I graduated high school, I was sixteen years old. As soon as I turned seventeen years old, I joined the United States Army. I made this decision because I wanted to become independent and because I also knew my mother did not have the financial means to afford my college education. The military offered me hope to acquire a college education. Fast-forward approximately twelve years later, after coming from a deployment in Afghanistan I decided to acquire my first property in the Dominican Republic where my family is originally from. It was here where I discovered my passion in hospitality. I furnished this property and started offering short-term rentals to tourists who wished to come visit the second biggest city in the Dominican Republic, Santiago de Los Caballeros. I now manage a total of ten properties and run my own company.

I look to continue growing this company and others with the knowledge I acquire in my graduate degree of Entrepreneurship and Innovation. Through this course I also look to gain the most knowledge in hospitality to better serve my clients and those who seek my expertise. My mother's struggle was my motivation to always strive to become as great as I can be. I look forward to a great semester as I approach the end of my graduate degree.

## Digital Story #3

In our household, education was never regarded as a priority for females. Why do we need to be educated to be able to clean the house or cook food or even to take care of our children? I began a journey to become the independent and educated woman I am now, breaking out from the misogynistic environment that my family and generations before them established and believed. I am now the first individual in my entire bloodline, the first female, to be admitted into one of the best universities for a master's program where I will continue my studies.

I have been traveling over the world since I can remember. I have stayed in hundreds of hotels and experienced the overall satisfaction of excellent service. Being able to create an unforgettable encounter inspired me to want to be able to do the same for others. I would like to start a business in the food and beverage industry as well as event planning and work hand in hand in both careers.

I graduated with a bachelor's degree in hospitality management from St. John's University. Continuing my education at SJU to get a Master of Science in International Hospitality Management was the ideal way to kick-start my profession and pave the way to success. This program will allow me to expand my managerial hospitality knowledge and offer me more behind the scenes information.

## Digital Story #4

My name is Juliet and I'm a junior here at St. John's University. Going into college I didn't really know what I wanted to major in or even what I wanted to do with my life. In my freshman and sophomore years, I took a lot of different classes in order to get a better understanding of what I liked and didn't like. Most of those classes within their majors didn't feel like the right fit for me. In the spring semester of my sophomore year, I took hospitality management along with food and beverage service and found it really interesting. From then on, I decided to declare my major in hospitality because it was one of the only majors that I gravitated to.

I've lived in Queens, New York my whole life and my family consists of my dad, my mom, and my younger brother, Brendan, who's nine years old. My brother is such a big part of my life and I love having him around. He and I always make time to watch YouTube videos, shows, and movies together. In my free time I also love to go to the gym. Lifting is something that I have become very passionate about and has become a form of therapy for me. I love incorporating fitness into my life and other people's lives, which is why I decided to become a personal trainer.

Aside from my home life, I'm excited to get back into school life because being a hospitality major makes my classes a lot more enjoyable. I'm eager for this class in particular because I'll get to do more research on a different country and learn more about it. My family is from Puerto Rico so I don't really have much knowledge about countries outside of the U.S.

These are all great stories. They're from the heart, often poignant, and many of them make me cry. There are many more stories like these. I like to use this exercise as a way for students to understand that they are a brand. They need to know who they are, what they're good at and enjoy doing, and what their limitations are. The first step to being employed is self-awareness, and the second step is knowing how to market yourself. Digital storytelling helps them understand that.

The most rewarding aspect of what I do is engaging students by sharing experiences, which become teachable moments. It's at that point where I as a professor learn as much if not more, from my students than they learn from me.

This book is my story and the many lessons I've learned along the way. I never in my wildest dreams thought I would publish a book. If it wasn't for academia, I don't think I would have told my story, but now as I write this last chapter, I am so glad I did.

In a way it's been therapy, throwing my life on a screen, and not only writing my own movie but reviewing it too. It's helped me realize you can't go forward until you've really seen the patterns in your past. Understanding your life gives you a chance to see what direction you're going in. Writing this book has helped me crystallize where I've been, where I am now, and where I'm going.

I could never have imagined when I graduated from St. John's in 1975 that someday I would return in a teaching role and that I would have my own travel business. And yet, here I am in my fourteenth year in academia and this year Gutsy Women Travel celebrates our twentieth year. I have met so many amazing women over the years, many of whom have become friends. I've had adventures and experiences that could fill two lifetimes.

Throughout this book, I've mentioned the angels who have been there for me along the way, opening doors at just the right time. I'm so glad I walked through them. I truly believe we all have angels in life, but often we don't recognize them. When you stay open to possibilities, when you ask for help, when you learn to say yes, and take a leap of faith, you will find your angels.

I am very grateful to live a life I am passionate about and doing the things I love—traveling the world, providing women and entrepreneurs with empowering experiences, mentoring young people, and getting them excited about the field of hospitality as well as their own career path.

This is my story. Thanks for taking the journey with me.

Remember: **It's Your Life...Live IT!**

# *Acknowledgements*

Throughout the pages of this book, I have mentioned the many, many people, including several of my angels who have been so important in my life. I thank you all.

In addition, I would like to thank:

Pat Wilson, the consummate literary guru who has reviewed my writings over the years and always provides poignant feedback to help my progress.

Dick Basmagy, a marketing genius who helped design the beautiful cover of this book and who assembled the one hundred photos and captions in our photo gallery.

Josh Blaisdell, web software developer at Eagre Web Solutions who has been our Gutsy Women Travel webmaster since 2006. We are deeply indebted to his masterful development of our coveted www.gutsywomentravel.com website.

Cheryl Benton, my editor and publisher for believing in my story and enabling it to be shared with others. I appreciate her guidance, support, and patience every step along the way in making my book a reality.

*April M. Merenda*

# *About the author*

**April Merenda** has held key positions within the hospitality and tourism industry over the past four decades, most notably being the co-founder of Gutsy Women Travel, LLC, the largest niche marketing company promoting travel designed for women and their unique interest. April is highly regarded for her high energy and hands-on approach to business development and has solidified major industry relationships within the hospitality industry.

She is the daughter of an Italian immigrant family from Salerno, Italy and was born in Brooklyn, New York. She earned her bachelor's of science and her master's in Leadership Management at St. John's University, located in Queens, NY. She taught as an adjunct professor within the Hospitality Management program for twelve years while simultaneously being employed as an assistant to the dean/external affairs for the College of Professional Studies. April is currently an assistant professor/industry professional tenure-track within St. John's University Hospitality Management program and brings a wealth of industry experience and networking opportunities to the classroom. She is also a member of The McCallen Society, a community of alumni benefactors and friends. She recently accepted the position of program coordinator for the new master's in science degree for International Hospitality Management, MSIHM, at St. John's University.

*It's Your Life...Live IT!* is her first book.

Made in USA - North Chelmsford, MA
1288966_9781737617730
11.09.2021 1611